The MAILBOX®
The Education Center®

Everything
Colors & Shapes

grades PreK-K

MW01156869

Timesaving tools for important skills practice

- **Practice pages**
- **Picture cards to sort**
- **Games**
- **Booklets**

- **Quick crafts**
- **Puppets**

Activities for 11 colors and 8 shapes!

Managing Editor: Kelly Robertson

Editorial Team: Becky S. Andrews, Diane Badden, Kimberley Bruck, Karen A. Brudnak, Pam Crane, Lynette Dickerson, Sarah Foreman, Pierce Foster, Ada Goren, Tazmen Hansen, Marsha Heim, Lori Z. Henry, Debra Liverman, Kitty Lowrance, Dorothy C. McKinney, Thad H. McLaurin, Brenda Miner, Sharon Murphy, Jennifer Nunn, Mark Rainey, Greg D. Rieves, Hope Rodgers, Eliseo De Jesus Santos II, Donna K. Teal, Rachael Traylor

www.themailbox.com

©2009 The Mailbox® Books
All rights reserved.
ISBN10 #1-56234-885-X • ISBN13 #978-156234-885-4

Printed in the United States
10 9 8 7 6 5 4 3 2 1

What's

color and shape illustrations

green

star

fun practice pages

Name _____

Turtle Likes Ovals

Trace.
Color.

fold-and-go booklets

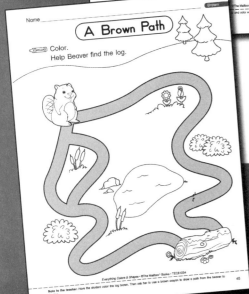

Name _____

A Brown Path

Color.
Help Beaver find the log.

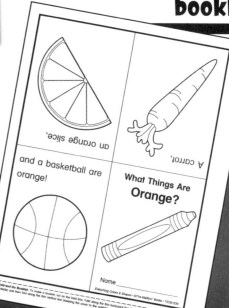

Inside

picture cards

Name _____

Color-O

games

red

MAIL

blue

quick crafts

Quick Craft

Fly, Dragon, Fly!

Materials: cotton batting (or cotton balls), crayons or markers, glue

Directions: Draw and color triangular scales along the upper edge of the dragon, from its head to the tip of its tail. Then color the rest of the dragon and the sky. Spread glue on the cloud shape. Press cotton batting on the glue.

Everything Colors & Shapes • ©The Mailbox® Books • TEC61234

Triangles

puppets

Table of Contents

red

a firetruck,

A barn,

and an apple are red!

What Things Are Red?

Name _____

Everything Colors & Shapes • ©The Mailbox® Books • TEC61234

Fold-and-Go Booklet: To make a booklet, cut on the bold line. Fold along the thin horizontal line (keeping the programming to the outside) and then fold along the thin vertical line (keeping the cover to the outside).

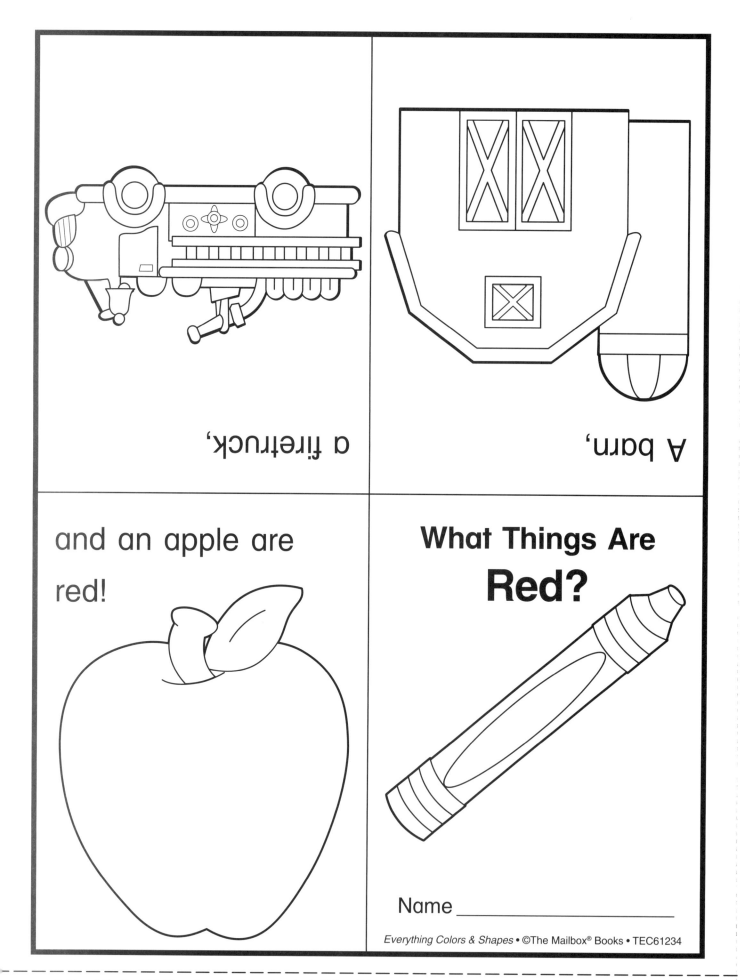

Red

_____ likes

red

Class Book Page: Write a child's name on the line. Then read aloud the sentence starter and ask the student to use a red crayon to draw and color one or more favorite red things. Label the drawing with the youngster's words. Publish the pages in a class book titled "Our Favorite Red Things."

Name _____

Lion's Red Load

Color.
Cut.
Glue.

Everything Colors & Shapes • ©The Mailbox® Books • TEC61234

Note to the teacher: Have the child use a red crayon to color the circle on the truck cab and the pictured items that are normally red. Then have him cut out the pictures and glue on the truck the ones that belong in Lion's red load.

A Red Path

Color.

Help Mouse find the strawberries.

Note to the teacher: Have the student color the strawberries red. Then ask her to use a red crayon to draw a path from the mouse to the strawberries.

Red Ladybug Puppet

To make a stick puppet, color the artwork red and then cut on the bold line. Fold along the thin horizontal line (keeping the artwork to the outside). Tape one end of a jumbo craft stick between the folded paper and then glue.

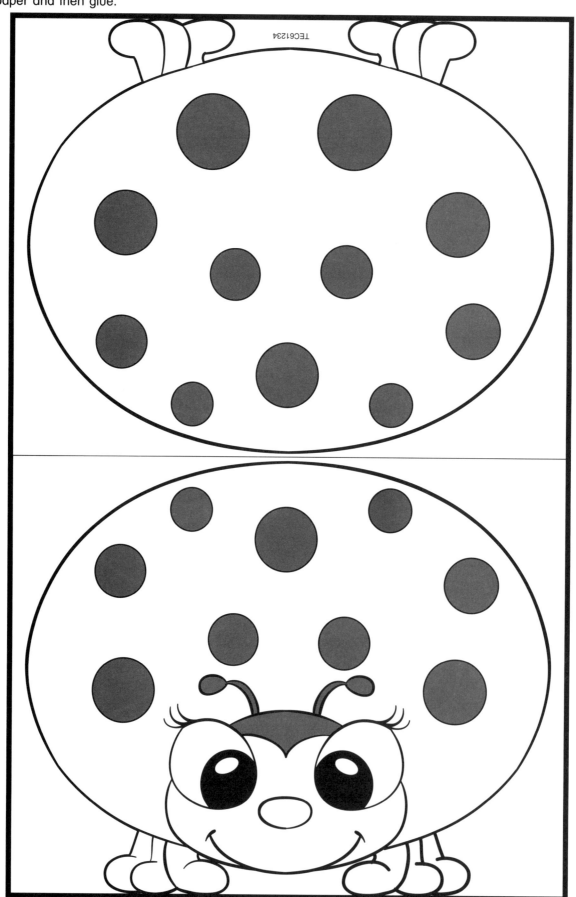

Everything Colors & Shapes • ©The Mailbox® Books • TEC61234

yellow

a daffodil,

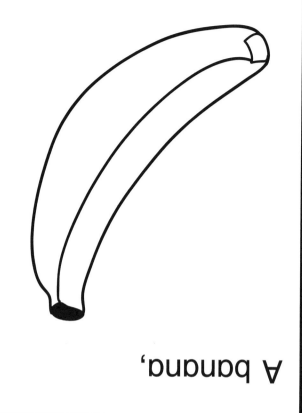

A banana,

and an ear of corn
are yellow!

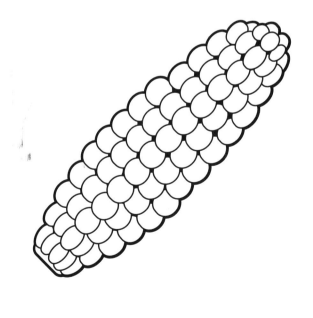

What Things Are
Yellow?

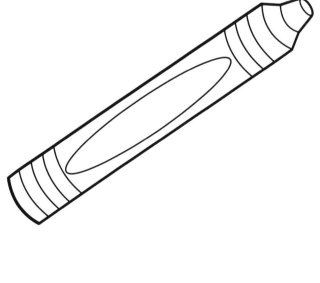

Name _____

Everything Colors & Shapes • ©The Mailbox® Books • TEC61234

Yellow

_____ likes

yellow

Everything Colors & Shapes • ©The Mailbox® Books • TEC61234

Class Book Page: Write a child's name on the line. Then read aloud the sentence starter and ask the student to use a yellow crayon to draw and color one or more favorite yellow things. Label the drawing with the youngster's words. Publish the pages in a class book titled "Our Favorite Yellow Things."

Lion's Yellow Load

Color.

Cut.

Glue.

Everything Colors & Shapes • ©The Mailbox® Books • TEC61234

Note to the teacher: Have the child use a yellow crayon to color the circle on the truck cab and the pictured items that are normally yellow. Then have him cut out the pictures and glue on the truck the ones that belong in Lion's yellow load.

Name _____

A Yellow Path

Color.

Help Monkey find the bananas.

Everything Colors & Shapes • ©The Mailbox® Books • TEC61234

Note to the teacher: Have the student color the bananas yellow. Then ask her to use a yellow crayon to draw a path from the monkey to the bananas.

15

Yellow Duck Puppet

To make a stick puppet, color the artwork and cut on the bold line. Fold along the thin horizontal line (keeping the artwork to the outside). Tape one end of a jumbo craft stick between the folded paper and then glue.

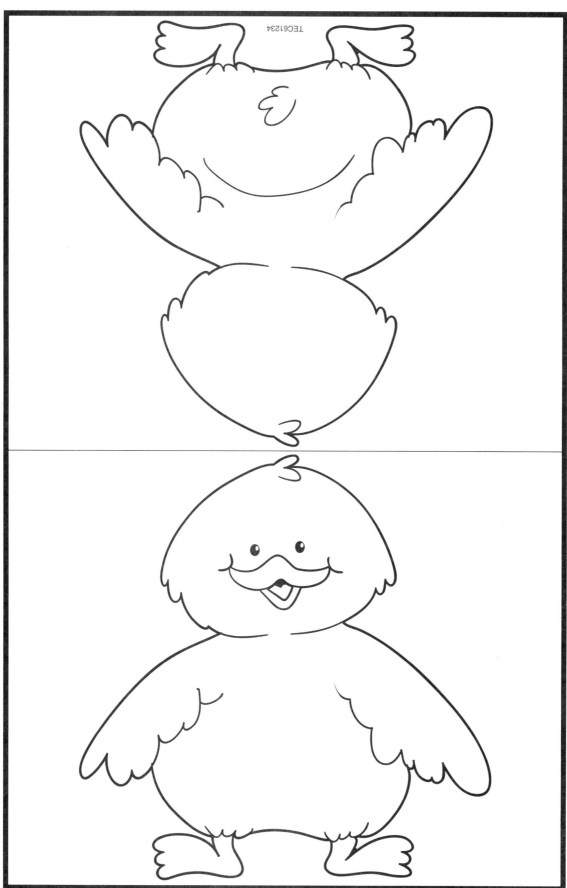

Everything Colors & Shapes • ©The Mailbox® Books • TEC61234

blue

a mailbox,

A blueberry,

and a bluebird are blue!

What Things Are
Blue?

Name _____

Everything Colors & Shapes • ©The Mailbox® Books • TEC61234

Fold-and-Go Booklet: To make a booklet, cut on the bold line. Fold along the thin horizontal line (keeping the programming to the outside) and then fold along the thin vertical line (keeping the cover to the outside).

Blue

_____ likes

blue

Everything Colors & Shapes • ©The Mailbox® Books • TEC61234

Class Book Page: Write a child's name on the line. Then read aloud the sentence starter and ask the student to use a blue crayon to draw and color one or more favorite blue things. Label the drawing with the youngster's words. Publish the pages in a class book titled "Our Favorite Blue Things."

Lion's Blue Load

Color.

Cut.

Glue.

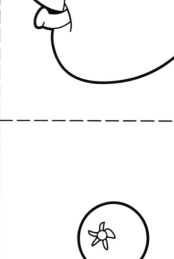

Everything Colors & Shapes • ©The Mailbox® Books • TEC61234

Note to the teacher: Have the child use a blue crayon to color the circle on the truck cab and the pictured items that are normally blue. Then have him cut out the pictures and glue on the truck the ones that belong in Lion's blue load.

A Blue Path

Color.

Help Kitty find the mailbox.

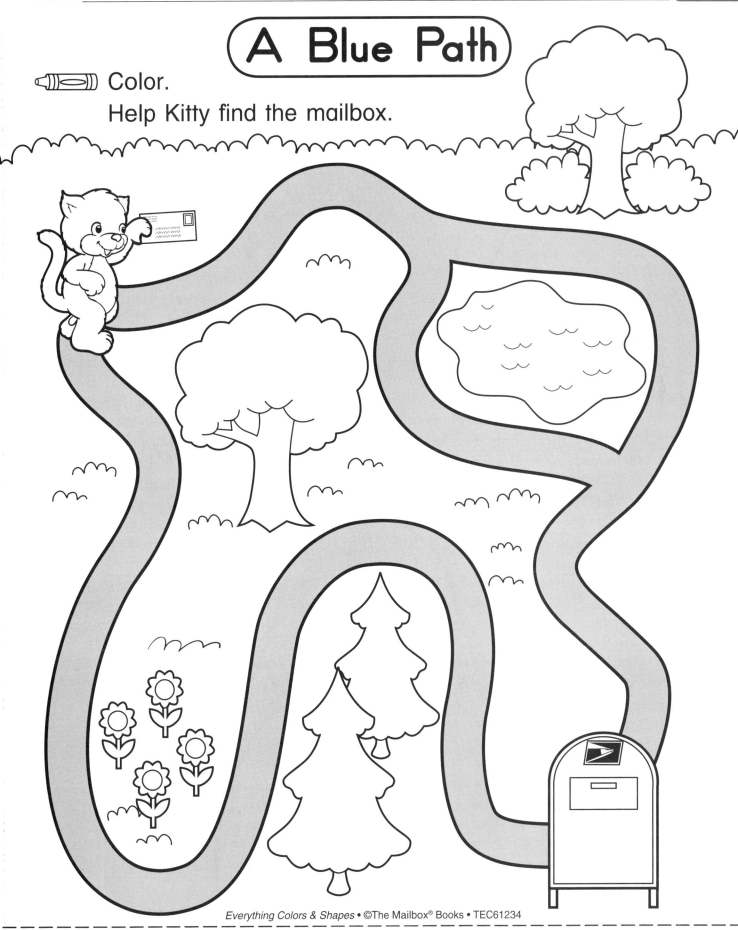

Everything Colors & Shapes • ©The Mailbox® Books • TEC61234

Note to the teacher: Have the student color the mailbox blue. Then ask her to use a blue crayon to draw a path from the kitten to the mailbox.

Blue Bluebird Puppet

To make a stick puppet, color the artwork and cut on the bold line. Fold along the thin horizontal line (keeping the artwork to the outside). Tape one end of a jumbo craft stick between the folded paper and then glue.

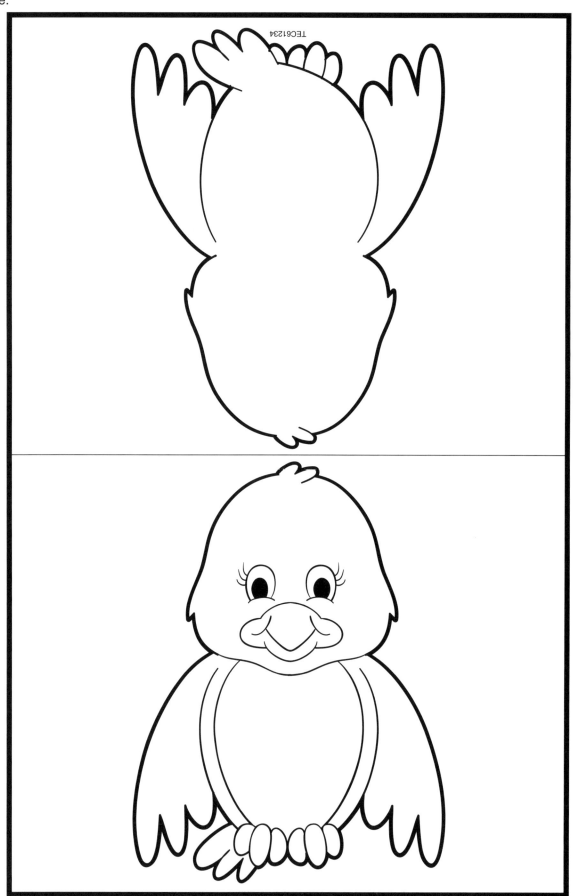

Everything Colors & Shapes • ©The Mailbox® Books • TEC61234

orange

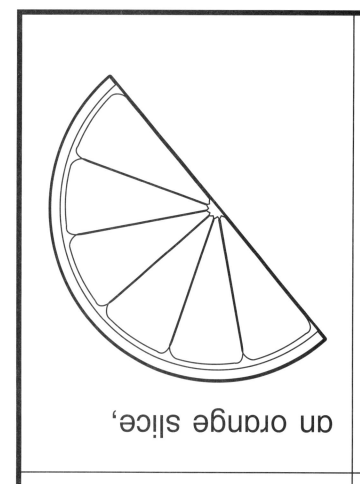

an orange slice,

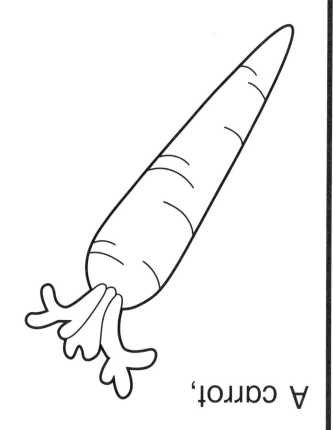

A carrot,

and a basketball are orange!

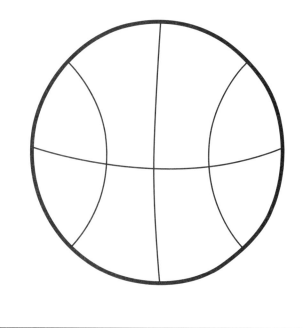

What Things Are
Orange?

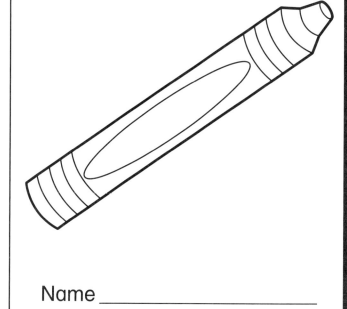

Name _____

Everything Colors & Shapes • ©The Mailbox® Books • TEC61234

Fold-and-Go Booklet: To make a booklet, cut on the bold line. Fold along the thin horizontal line (keeping the programming to the outside) and then fold along the thin vertical line (keeping the cover to the outside).

Orange

_____ likes

orange

Class Book Page: Write a child's name on the line. Then read aloud the sentence starter and ask the student to use an orange crayon to draw and color one or more favorite orange things. Label the drawing with the youngster's words. Publish the pages in a class book titled "Our Favorite Orange Things."

Name _____

26

Lion's Orange Load

Color.

Cut.

Glue.

Everything Colors & Shapes • ©The Mailbox® Books • TEC61234

Note to the teacher: Have the child use an orange crayon to color the circle on the truck cab and the pictured items that are normally orange. Then have him cut out the pictures and glue on the truck the ones that belong in Lion's orange load.

Name _____

An Orange Path

Color.

Help Bear find the oranges.

Everything Colors & Shapes • ©The Mailbox® Books • TEC61234

Note to the teacher: Have the student color the oranges orange. Then ask her to use an orange crayon to draw a path from the bear to the orange tree.

Orange Tiger Puppet

To make a stick puppet, color the artwork and cut on the bold line. Fold along the thin horizontal line (keeping the artwork to the outside). Tape one end of a jumbo craft stick between the folded paper and then glue.

Everything Colors & Shapes • ©The Mailbox® Books • TEC61234

green

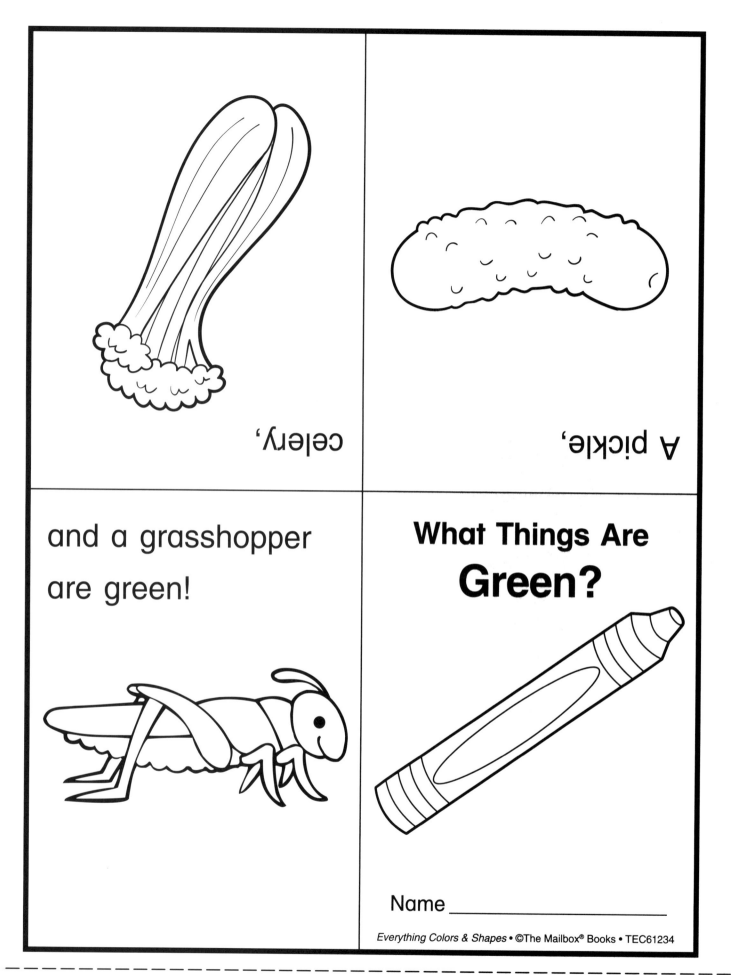

celery,

A pickle,

and a grasshopper
are green!

What Things Are
Green?

Name _____

Fold-and-Go Booklet: To make a booklet, cut on the bold line. Fold along the thin horizontal line (keeping the programming to the outside) and then fold along the thin vertical line (keeping the cover to the outside).

Green

_____ likes

green

Class Book Page: Write a child's name on the line. Then read aloud the sentence starter and ask the student to use a green crayon to draw and color one or more favorite green things. Label the drawing with the youngster's words. Publish the pages in a class book titled "Our Favorite Green Things."

Name _____

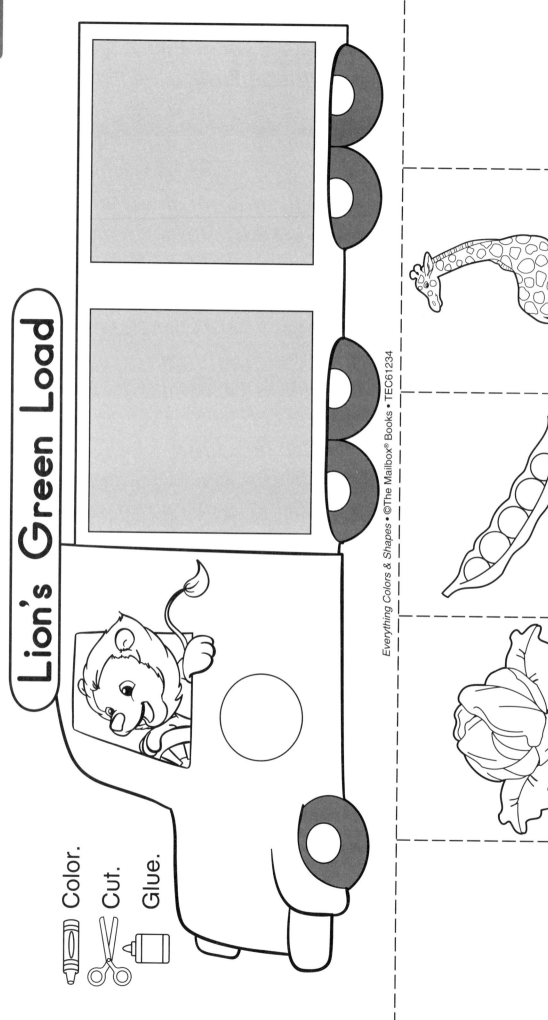

Lion's Green Load

Color.

Cut.

Glue.

Everything Colors & Shapes • ©The Mailbox® Books • TEC61234

Note to the teacher: Have the child use a green crayon to color the circle on the truck cab and the pictured items that are normally green. Then have him cut out the pictures and glue on the truck the ones that belong in Lion's green load.

A Green Path

Color.

Help Lizard find the cactus.

Everything Colors & Shapes • ©The Mailbox® Books • TEC61234

Note to the teacher: Have the student color the cactus green. Then ask her to use a green crayon to draw a path from the lizard to the cactus.

Green Alligator Puppet

To make a stick puppet, color the artwork and cut on the bold line. Fold along the thin horizontal line (keeping the artwork to the outside). Tape one end of a jumbo craft stick between the folded paper and then glue.

TEC61234

purple

a violet,

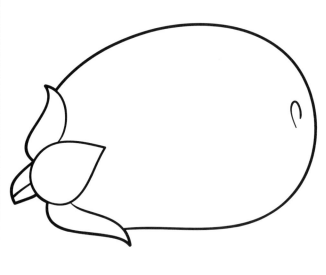

An eggplant,

and a plum are
purple!

What Things Are
Purple?

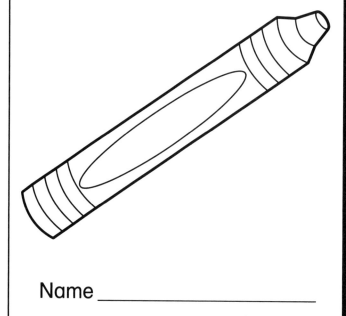

Name _____

Everything Colors & Shapes • ©The Mailbox® Books • TEC61234

Fold-and-Go Booklet: To make a booklet, cut on the bold line. Fold along the thin horizontal line (keeping the programming to the outside) and then fold along the thin vertical line (keeping the cover to the outside).

Purple

_____ likes

purple

Class Book Page: Write a child's name on the line. Then read aloud the sentence starter and ask the student to use a purple crayon to draw and color one or more favorite purple things. Label the drawing with the youngster's words. Publish the pages in a class book titled "Our Favorite Purple Things."

Lion's Purple Load

Color.

Cut.

Glue.

Everything Colors & Shapes • ©The Mailbox® Books • TEC61234

Note to the teacher: Have the child use a purple crayon to color the circle on the truck cab and the pictured items that are normally purple. Then have him cut out the pictures and glue on the truck the ones that belong in Lion's purple load.

Name_____

A Purple Path

Color.

Help Bunny find the violets.

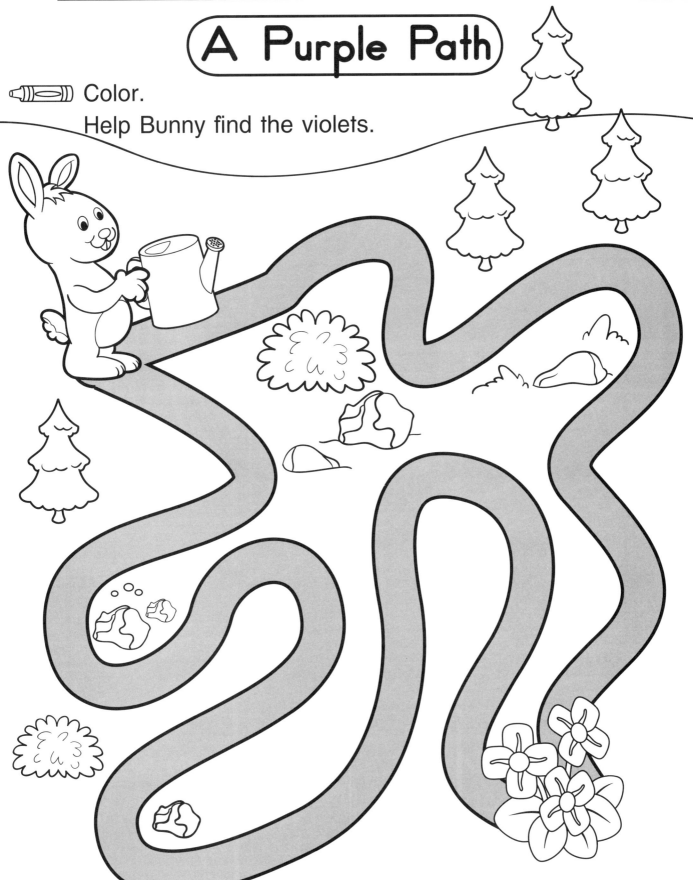

Everything Colors & Shapes • ©The Mailbox® Books • TEC61234

Note to the teacher: Have the student color the violets purple. Then ask her to use a purple crayon to draw a path from the bunny to the violets.

39

Purple Jellyfish Puppet

To make a stick puppet, color the artwork and cut on the bold line. Fold along the thin horizontal line (keeping the artwork to the outside). Tape one end of a jumbo craft stick between the folded paper and then glue.

Everything Colors & Shapes • ©The Mailbox® Books • TEC61234

brown

a pretzel,

A football,

and a pinecone are brown!

What Things Are
Brown?

Name _____

Everything Colors & Shapes • ©The Mailbox® Books • TEC61234

Fold-and-Go Booklet: To make a booklet, cut on the bold line. Fold along the thin horizontal line (keeping the programming to the outside) and then fold along the thin vertical line (keeping the cover to the outside).

Brown

_____ likes

brown

Everything Colors & Shapes • ©The Mailbox® Books • TEC61234

Class Book Page: Write a child's name on the line. Then read aloud the sentence starter and ask the student to use a brown crayon to draw and color one or more favorite brown things. Label the drawing with the youngster's words. Publish the pages in a class book titled "Our Favorite Brown Things."

Name

44

Lion's Brown Load

Color.
Cut.
Glue.

Everything Colors & Shapes • ©The Mailbox® Books • TEC61234

Note to the teacher: Have the child use a brown crayon to color the circle on the truck cab and the pictured items that are normally brown. Then have him cut out the pictures and glue on the truck the ones that belong in Lion's brown load.

A Brown Path

Color.

Help Beaver find the log.

Note to the teacher: Have the student color the log brown. Then ask her to use a brown crayon to draw a path from the beaver to the log.

Brown Bear Puppet

To make a stick puppet, color the artwork and cut on the bold line. Fold along the thin horizontal line (keeping the artwork to the outside). Tape one end of a jumbo craft stick between the folded paper and then glue.

Everything Colors & Shapes • ©The Mailbox® Books • TEC61234

pink

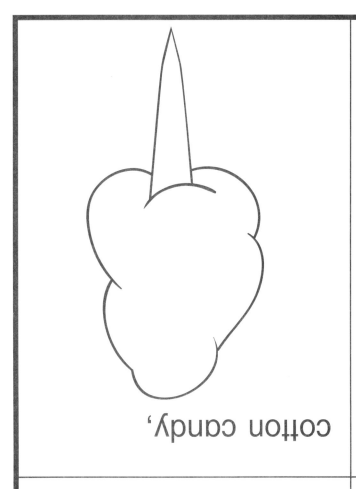

cotton candy,

A rose,

and a flamingo are pink!

What Things Are
Pink?

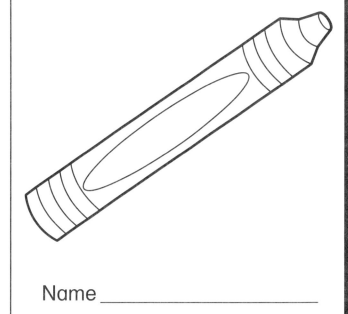

Name _____

Everything Colors & Shapes • ©The Mailbox® Books • TEC61234

Fold-and-Go Booklet: To make a booklet, cut on the bold line. Fold along the thin horizontal line (keeping the programming to the outside) and then fold along the thin vertical line (keeping the cover to the outside).

Pink

_____ likes

pink

Class Book Page: Write a child's name on the line. Then read aloud the sentence starter and ask the student to use a pink crayon to draw and color one or more favorite pink things. Label the drawing with the youngster's words. Publish the pages in a class book titled "Our Favorite Pink Things."

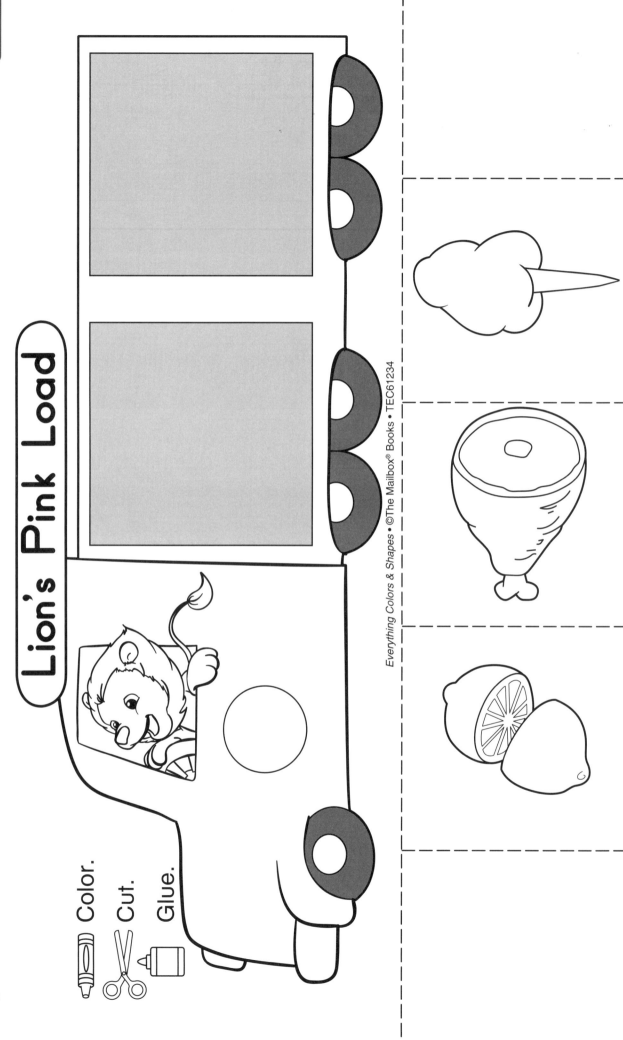

Name

Lion's Pink Load

Color.

Cut.

Glue.

Everything Colors & Shapes • ©The Mailbox® Books • TEC61234

Note to the teacher: Have the child use a pink crayon to color the circle on the truck cab and the pictured items that are normally pink. Then have him cut out the pictures and glue on the truck the ones that belong in Lion's pink load.

Name _____

A Pink Path

Color.
Help Farmer find Pig.

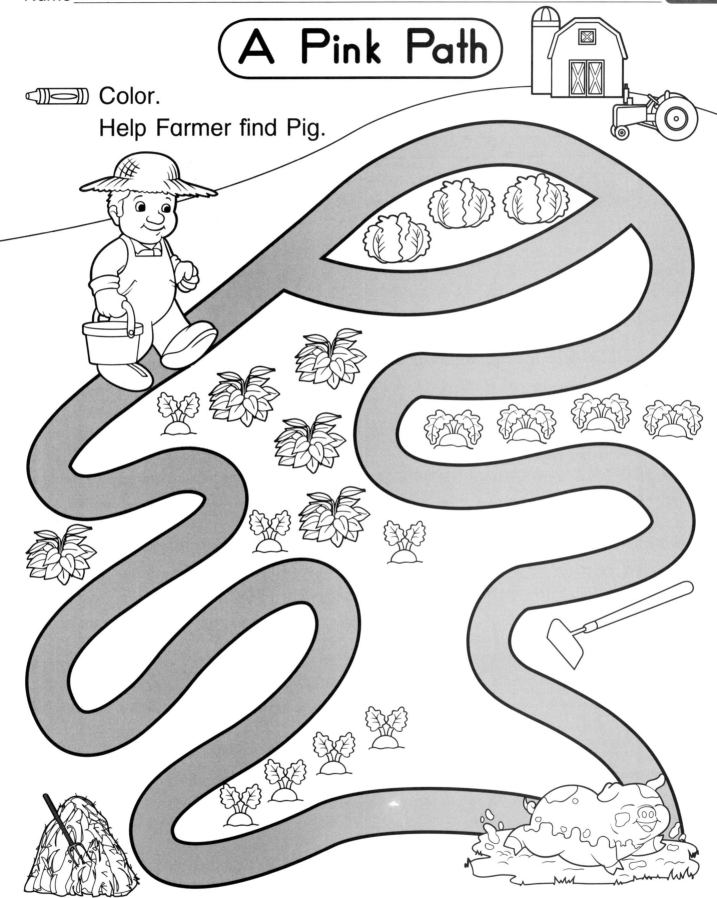

Note to the teacher: Have the student color the pig pink. Then ask her to use a pink crayon to draw a path from the farmer to the pig.

Pink Pig Puppet

To make a stick puppet, color the artwork and cut on the bold line. Fold along the thin horizontal line (keeping the artwork to the outside). Tape one end of a jumbo craft stick between the folded paper and then glue.

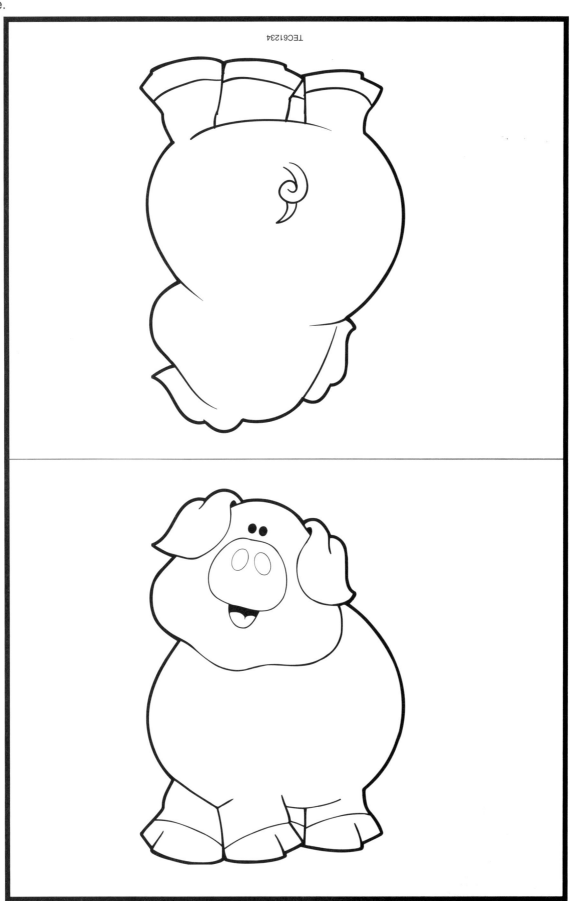

TEC61234

Everything Colors & Shapes • ©The Mailbox® Books • TEC61234

gray

‚uᴉɥdlop ɒ

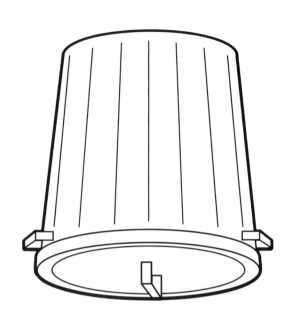

‚uɒɔ ǝƃɒqɹɒƃ A

and an elephant are gray!

What Things Are
Gray?

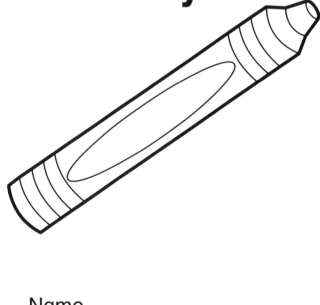

Name _____

Everything Colors & Shapes • ©The Mailbox® Books • TEC61234

Gray

_____ likes

gray

Everything Colors & Shapes • ©The Mailbox® Books • TEC61234

Class Book Page: Write a child's name on the line. Then read aloud the sentence starter and ask the student to use a gray crayon to draw and color one or more favorite gray things. Label the drawing with the youngster's words. Publish the pages in a class book titled "Our Favorite Gray Things."

Name

Lion's Gray Load

Color.

Cut.

Glue.

Everything Colors & Shapes • ©The Mailbox® Books • TEC61234

Note to the teacher: Have the child use a gray crayon to color the circle on the truck cab and the pictured items that are normally gray. Then have him cut out the pictures and glue on the truck the ones that belong in Lion's gray load.

A Gray Path

Color.

Help Mouse find the elephant.

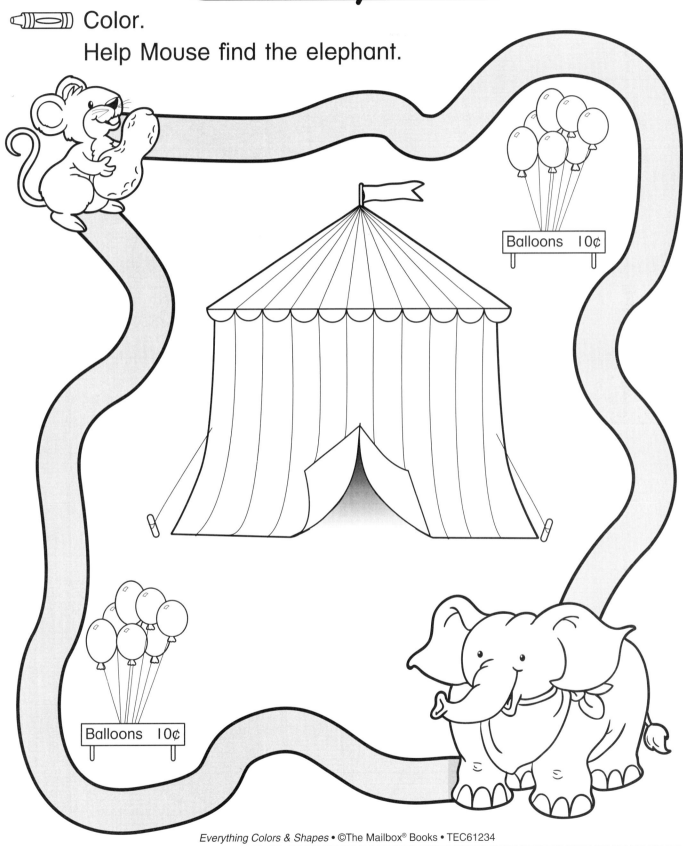

Balloons 10¢

Balloons 10¢

Note to the teacher: Have the student color the elephant gray. Then ask her to use a gray crayon to draw a path from the mouse to the elephant.

Gray Squirrel Puppet

To make a stick puppet, color the artwork and cut on the bold line. Fold along the thin horizontal line (keeping the artwork to the outside). Tape one end of a jumbo craft® stick between the folded paper and then glue.

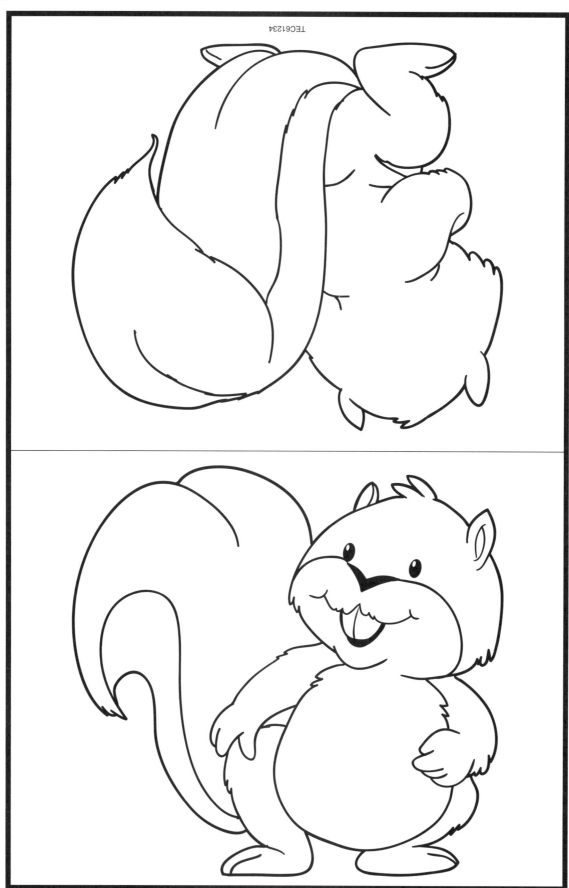

Everything Colors & Shapes • ©The Mailbox® Books • TEC61234

black
and **white**

a soccer ball,

A zebra,

and a panda are
black and white!

What Things Are
Black and White?

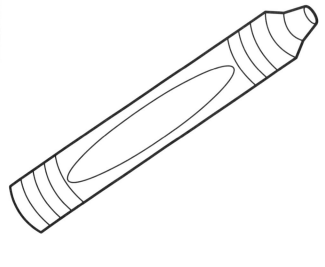

Name _____

Everything Colors & Shapes • ©The Mailbox® Books • TEC61234

Fold-and-Go Booklet: To make a booklet, cut on the bold line. Fold along the thin horizontal line (keeping the programming to the
outside) and then fold along the thin vertical line (keeping the cover to the outside).

Black and White

_____ likes

black and white

Class Book Page: Write a child's name on the line. Then read aloud the sentence starter and ask the student to use a black crayon and a white crayon to draw and color one or more favorite black and white things. Label the drawing with the youngster's words. Publish the pages in a class book titled "Our Favorite Black and White Things."

Name _____

62

Lion's Black and White Load

🖍 Color.

✂️ Cut.

🧴 Glue.

Everything Colors & Shapes • ©The Mailbox® Books • TEC61234

Note to the teacher: Have the child use a black crayon and a white crayon to color the circles on the truck cab and the pictured items that are normally black and white. Then have him cut out the pictures and glue on the truck the ones that belong in Lion's black and white load.

A Black and White Path

Color.

Help Farmer find Cow.

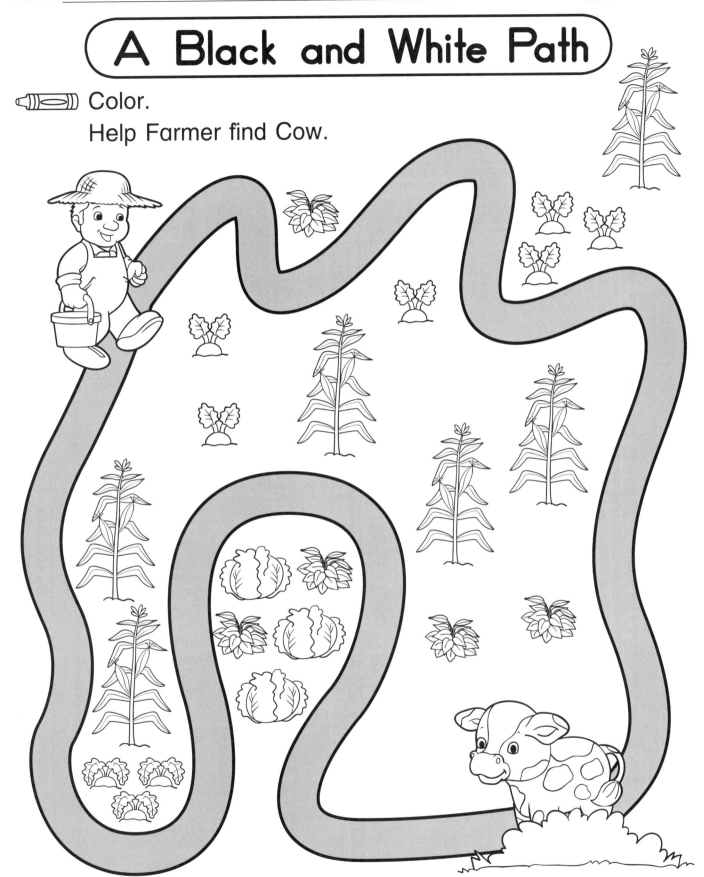

Everything Colors & Shapes • ©The Mailbox® Books • TEC61234

Note to the teacher: Have the student color the cow's spots black. Then ask her to use a black crayon and a white crayon to draw a black path and a white path from the farmer to the cow.

Black and White Panda Puppet

To make a stick puppet, color the artwork and cut on the bold line. Fold along the thin horizontal line (keeping the artwork to the outside). Tape one end of a jumbo craft stick between the folded paper and then glue.

Color-O Games

Pages 65 and 66

Preparing and playing the games:

To prepare, give each child a copy of a gameboard from this page or page 66. Each student also needs the following crayons: red, yellow, blue, orange, green, purple, brown, pink, gray, and black. Use the gameboards for a variety of coloring games. (Select pictures on each card may be colored in more than one way.) Possible games include the following:

• Find and Color

Name a color. A child finds a picture on his gameboard that can be the color and uses the matching crayon to color the picture. Invite little ones to explain their selections. Continue playing until each player has colored several pictures.

• Tic-Tac-Color

Name a color. A child finds a picture on her gameboard that can be the named color and uses the matching crayon to color the picture. The first player to color three pictures in a row wins.

• Cornered!

Name a color. A child finds a picture on his gameboard that can be the named color and uses the matching crayon to color the picture. The first player to color each corner picture wins.

Gameboard
Use with the directions on this page.

Everything Colors & Shapes • ©The Mailbox® Books • TEC61234

Gameboards
Use with the directions on page 65.

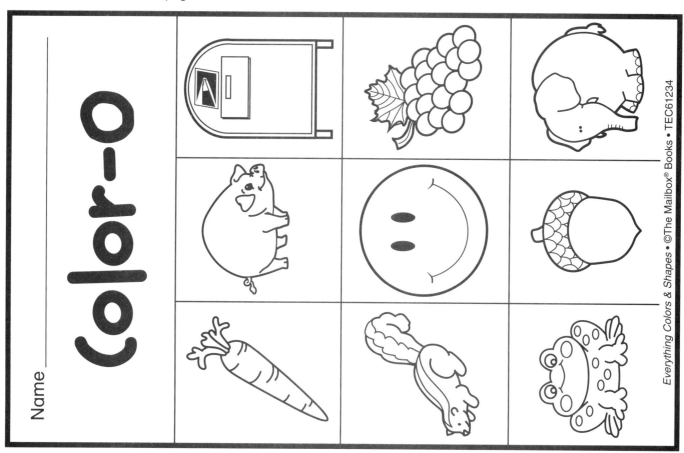

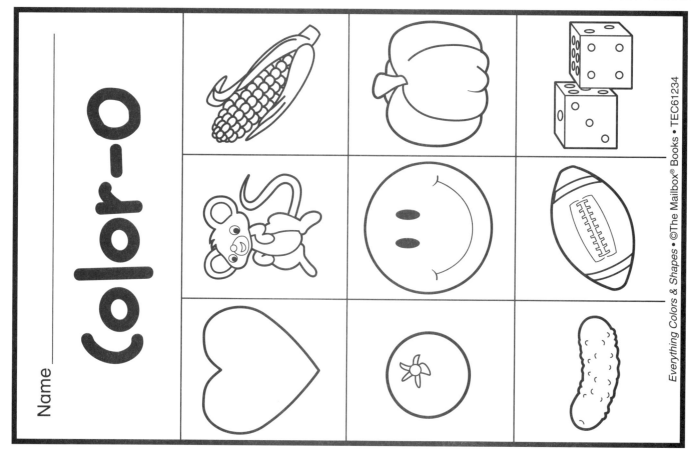

66

Crayon and Picture Cards

Pages 67–72

Preparing and using the cards:

Make a white construction paper copy of the cards on pages 68–72. Underline each color word on the crayon cards with the corresponding color of marker or crayon (or color one or both ends of each crayon picture). Then cut out the crayon cards and picture cards and use them as desired to reinforce a variety of skills. Possible activities include

- **Color recognition:** Say each color word. Ask a child to find the crayon card marked with the matching color.

- **Print awareness:** Say each color word. Ask a child to find the crayon card marked with the matching color and point to the color word.

- **Color identification:** Ask a child to point to each of several crayon cards and use the color-coding to name the individual colors.

- **Color awareness:** Have a child match picture cards to crayon cards based on color.

- **Color awareness:** Have a child match picture cards to picture cards based on color.

- **Word recognition:** Make an extra copy of the crayon cards. Cut out the cards. Say each color word. Ask a child to find the crayon card with the matching color word. Or have a child match each color-coded crayon card to a crayon card without color coding.

Bonus! Use the picture cards to play a variety of memory games. If desired, use the happy face cards as wild cards. To use a wild card, a player must name an item that matches the color of its partner card. If two wild cards are turned over, a player must name a color and two objects of that color.

Crayon Cards

Use with the directions on page 67.

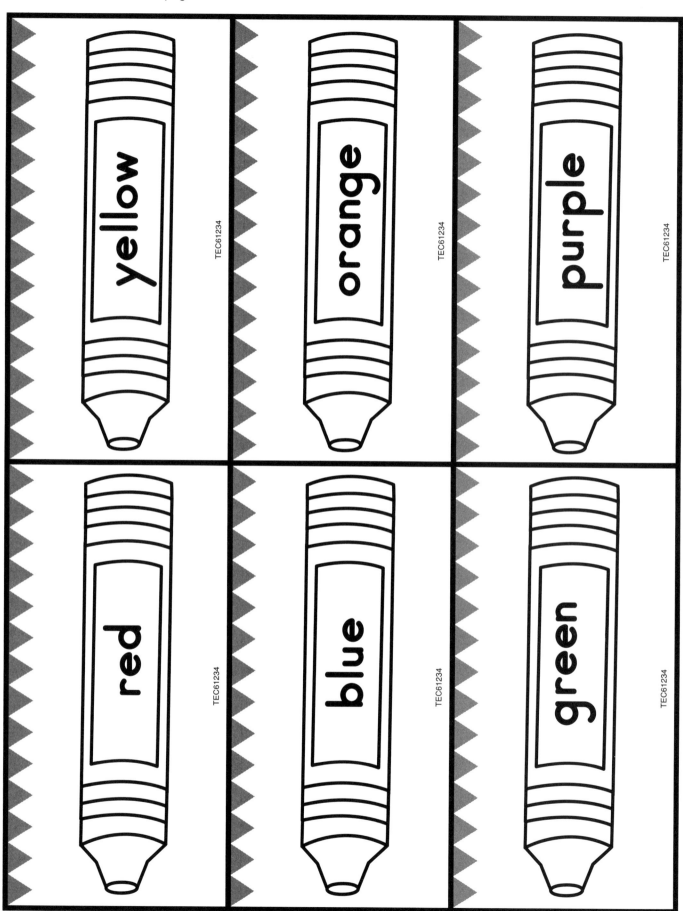

yellow

TEC61234

orange

TEC61234

purple

TEC61234

red

TEC61234

blue

TEC61234

green

TEC61234

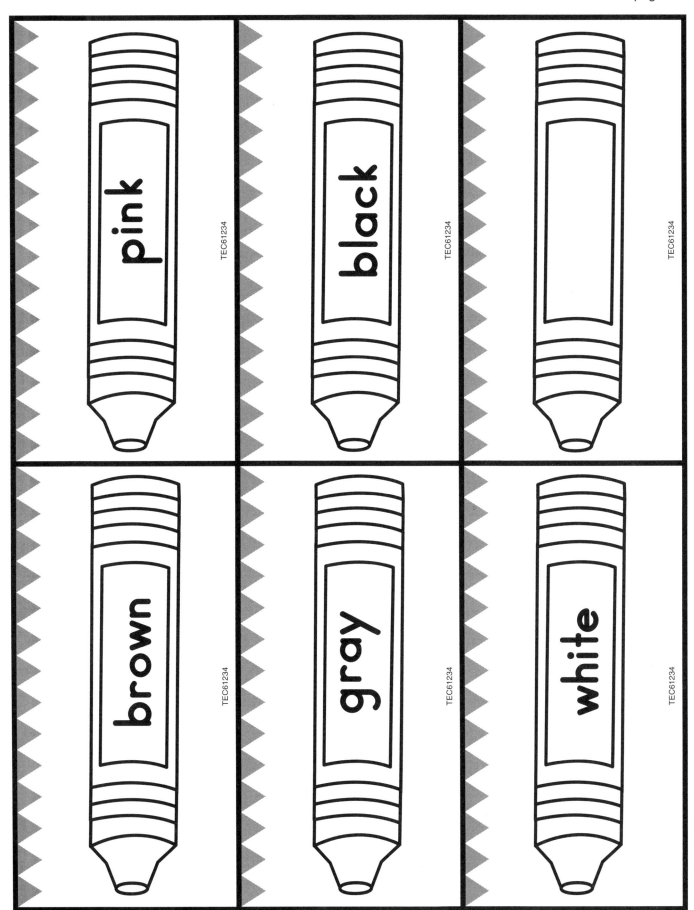

pink

TEC61234

black

TEC61234

TEC61234

brown

TEC61234

gray

TEC61234

white

TEC61234

Picture Cards

Use with the directions on page 67.

yellow
TEC61234

yellow
TEC61234

red
TEC61234

blue
TEC61234

blue
TEC61234

red
TEC61234

green
TEC61234

green
TEC61234

orange
TEC61234

orange
TEC61234

purple
TEC61234

purple
TEC61234

pink
TEC61234

pink
TEC61234

brown
TEC61234

gray
TEC61234

gray
TEC61234

brown
TEC61234

Picture and Wild Cards

Use with the directions on page 67.

black
TEC61234

black
TEC61234

white
TEC61234

white
TEC61234

Wild Card
TEC61234

Wild Card
TEC61234

Wild Card
TEC61234

Wild Card
TEC61234

Everything Colors & Shapes • ©The Mailbox® Books • TEC61234

Booklet-Making Activity

Pages 73–79

To prepare a booklet:

1. Copy on manila paper the booklet's front cover and inside back cover (page 74).
2. Then copy pages 75–79 on white paper.
3. Cut apart the covers and the pages.
4. Stack the pages between the covers.
5. Staple the left edge of the booklet.

To complete a booklet:

1. Help a child write her name on the front booklet cover. Then have her color the artwork.
2. Read aloud the color word on each page and on the inside back cover. Ask the child to use the matching-colored crayon to color the splotch. Next, have her trace and write the color word. Then ask her to draw something that is the named color.

Name _____

Everything Colors & Shapes • ©The Mailbox® Books • TEC61234

white

_____

- - - - - - - - - - - - - - - - - -

_____

Draw.

red

Draw.

yellow

Draw.

 blue

- - - - - - - - - - - - - - - - -

 orange

- - - - - - - - - - - - - - - - -

Draw.

_____

_ _

_____

Draw.

_____

_ _

_____

Draw.

_ _

_ _

Draw.

_____

- - - - - - - - - - - - - - - - - - - -

_____

🖍 Draw.

_____

- - - - - - - - - - - - - - - - - - - -

_____

🖍 Draw.

Name _____

80

Quack for Colors

Color.

Cut.

Glue.

yellow ◯

blue ◯

red ◯

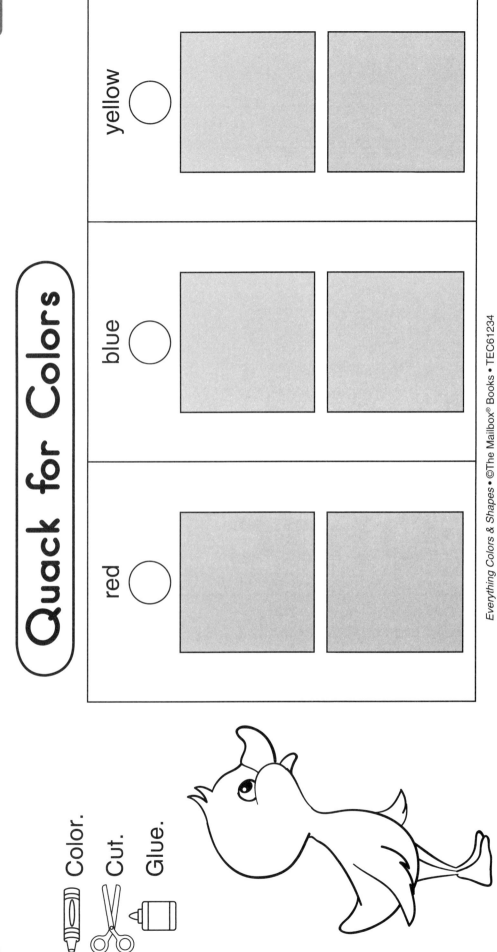

Everything Colors & Shapes • ©The Mailbox® Books • TEC61234

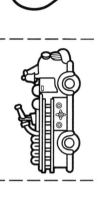

Note to the teacher: Help the student color each circle on the chart; then have her color and cut out the picture cards and glue them to the chart.

Name _____

Trucking Along!

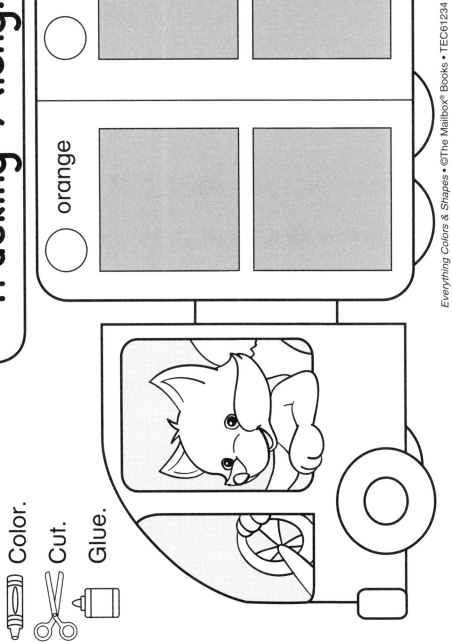

🖍 Color.

✂ Cut.

🧴 Glue.

brown ◯

green ◯

orange ◯

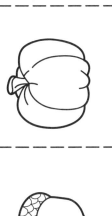

Everything Colors & Shapes • ©The Mailbox® Books • TEC61234

Note to the teacher: Help the student color each circle on the truck; then have him color and cut out the picture cards and glue them to the truck.

Name

Pelican's Pointer

Color.

Cut.

Glue.

○ white

○ pink

○ black

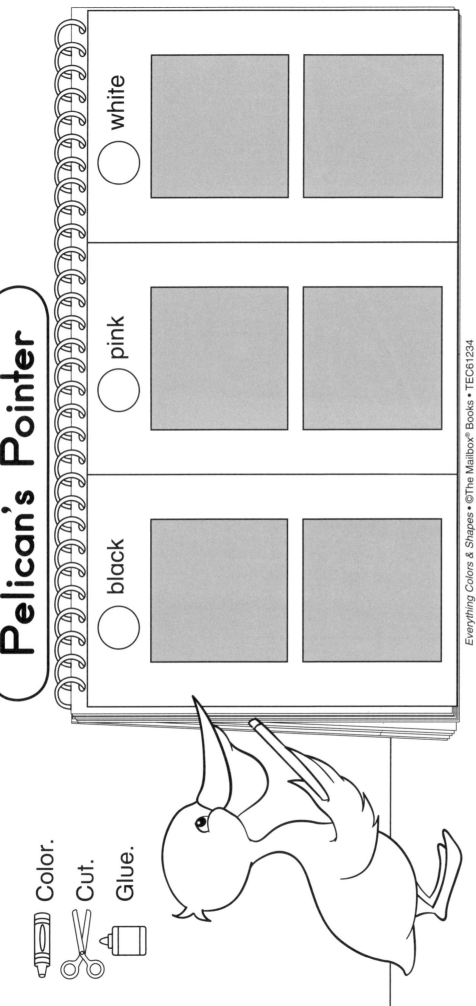

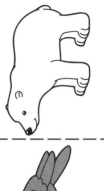

Everything Colors & Shapes • ©The Mailbox® Books • TEC61234

Note to the teacher: Help the student color each circle on the notepad; then have her color and cut out the picture cards and glue them to the notepad.

Name _____

Colorful Balloons!

Listen and do.

Note to the teacher: Have the student color two balloons pink, two balloons purple, one balloon yellow, and one balloon blue; then have him color the lion brown and the tiger orange.

Name

84

A Resting Place

Listen and do.

Everything Colors & Shapes • ©The Mailbox® Books • TEC61234

Note to the teacher: Have the student color the flower pink, the leaf green, the rock gray, and the log brown; then have her trace each dotted line with the matching color.

Name

Critters' Favorite Things

Listen and do.

Everything Colors & Shapes • ©The Mailbox® Books • TEC61234

Note to the teacher: Have the student color the pond blue, the barn red, the carrot orange, and the banana yellow; then have him trace each dotted line with the matching color.

85

Name

86

Laundry Day

Listen and do.

Everything Colors & Shapes • ©The Mailbox® Books • TEC61234

Note to the teacher: Have the student color the pants black, the shirt purple, the towel pink, and the squirrel gray. Then have her draw and color an article of clothing in the space provided, identifying the color she chooses.

Name_____

Mouse's House

 Color.

Color Code

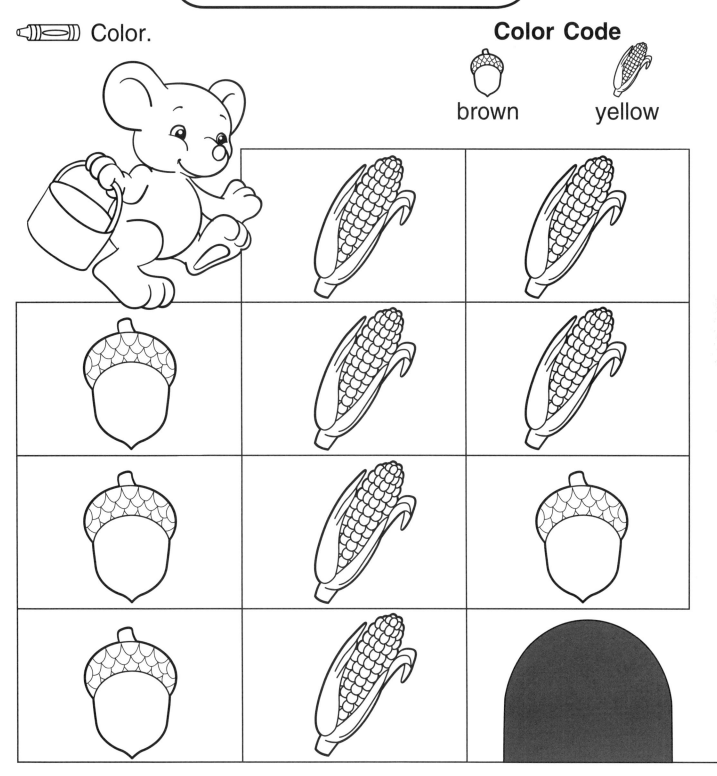

brown   yellow

Which item makes a path to Mouse's house?

 Circle the answer.

Everything Colors & Shapes • ©The Mailbox® Books • TEC61234

Turtle Goes to School

Color.

Color Code

green   red   purple

Which item takes Turtle to school?

 Circle the answer.

Everything Colors & Shapes • ©The Mailbox® Books • TEC61234

Note to the teacher: Help the student color each picture in the color code; then have her use the code to color the picture in each box.

Name _____

A Friendly Snake

🖍 Color.

Color Code

○ 1	○ 2
brown	yellow

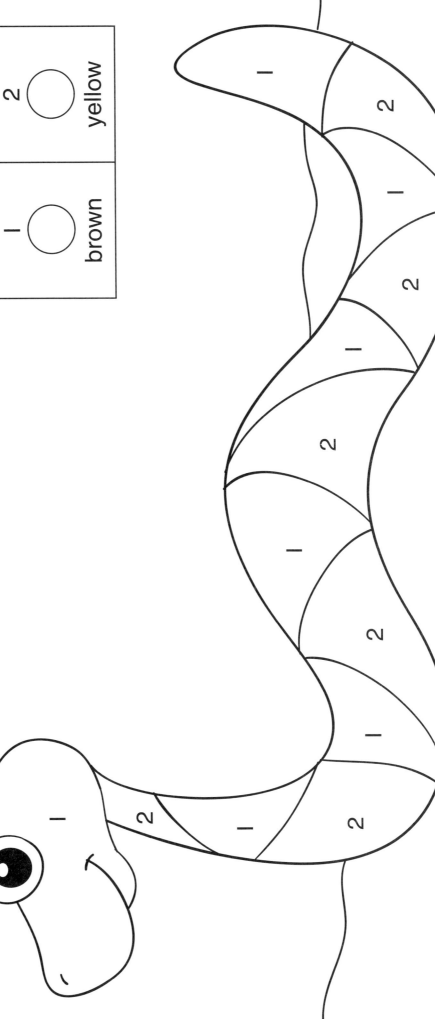

Everything Colors & Shapes • ©The Mailbox® Books • TEC61234

Note to the teacher: Help the student color each circle in the color code; then have him use the code to color the picture.

Name

Beautiful Fish

Color.

Color Code

1 pink
2 green
3 purple

Everything Colors & Shapes • ©The Mailbox® Books • TEC61234

Note to the teacher: Help the student color each circle in the color code; then have her use the code to color the picture.

Name

Cute Cackler

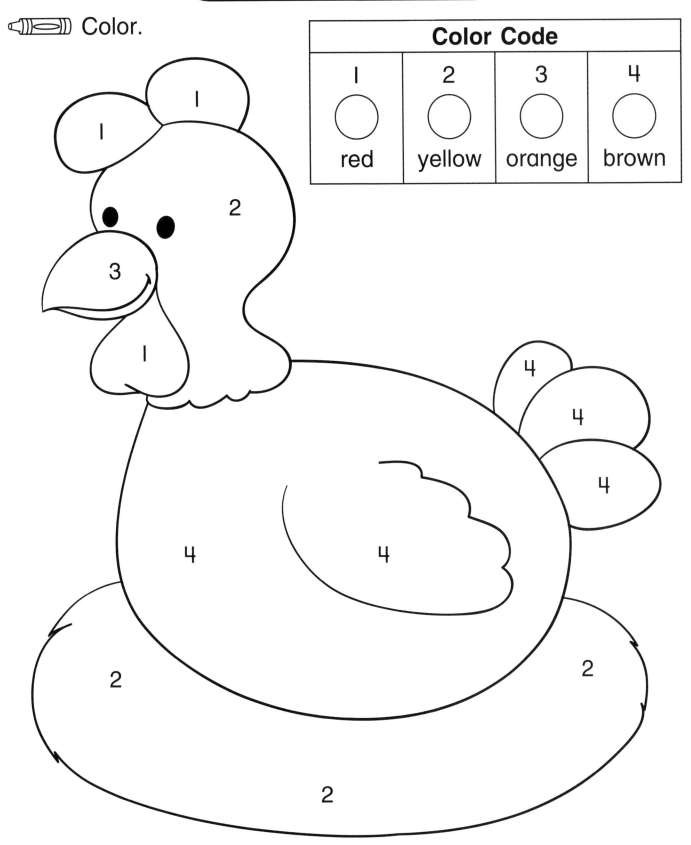

Color.

Color Code			
1	2	3	4
◯	◯	◯	◯
red	yellow	orange	brown

Note to the teacher: Help the student color each circle in the color code; then have him use the code to color the picture.

Full-Size Color Page

Large group: Copy a page on its matching-colored paper and glue it to a sheet of poster board. Have youngsters cut from magazines pictures of items that are the corresponding color. Invite each child to glue his cutouts to the poster board to make a colorful collage. **Color matching**

Center: Copy a page on its corresponding-colored paper and place it at a center along with manipulatives in a variety of colors. A child places the corresponding-colored items on the paper and sets the others aside. For an added challenge, use two or more mats and have students sort by more than one color. **Sorting by color**

Bonus Activities

Small group: Copy several different-colored pages onto their corresponding-colored paper and laminate them for durability. Attach the pages to the floor in an open area. A child stands a short distance away and tosses a beanbag toward the pages. Then she identifies the color that the beanbag lands on or closest to. **Color identification**

Fold-and-Go Booklet

Individual: Give each child a copy of a booklet and a long paper strip in the corresponding color. Have students color the pictures the appropriate color; then cut them out and glue them on the paper strip. Size each child's strip to his head and staple it to make a headband. **Color recognition**

Class Booklet Page

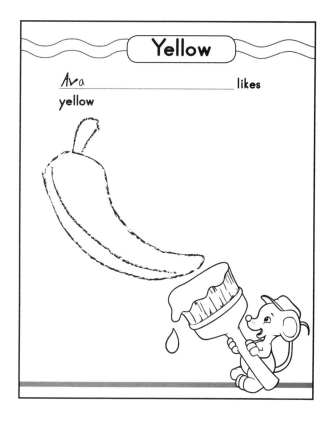

Small group: Give each student a copy of a class booklet page and help her write her name at the top. Announce clues about an object that is the corresponding color, such as "I'm thinking of a fruit. It has a peel. Monkeys like to eat it." Then have each child draw the item on her paper. **Critical thinking**

Partners: Give each child a copy of a class booklet page. Have one child in each pair name an object of the corresponding color for his partner to draw. Then have the partners switch roles. Continue until each child has a few drawings on his paper. **Color identification**

Bonus Activities

Maze

Center: Color the details at the start and finish of one copy of a maze, leaving the path uncolored. Laminate the page for durability. Place the maze at a center along with play dough in the corresponding color. A child rolls play dough into a snake shape and uses it to form the path on the maze. **Fine-motor skills**

Puppet

Small group: Prepare a desired puppet. Ask each child, in turn, to use the puppet as a pointer and point to something in the room that is the corresponding color. **Color recognition**

Red

Small group: Prepare a different-colored puppet for each child in a small group. Arrange the puppets in a circle on the floor in an open area. Play soft music as little ones walk around the circle. When you stop the music, each youngster picks up the puppet she is closest to. Then each child, in turn, names the color of her puppet. **Color identification**

Large group: Prepare puppets in several different colors. Have students sit in a circle; then give one child a puppet. Have him walk around the circle, gently tapping each child that is wearing the corresponding color as he says the color word aloud. Continue with different students and different-colored puppets. **Color recognition**

circle

Shape Cards: Circles

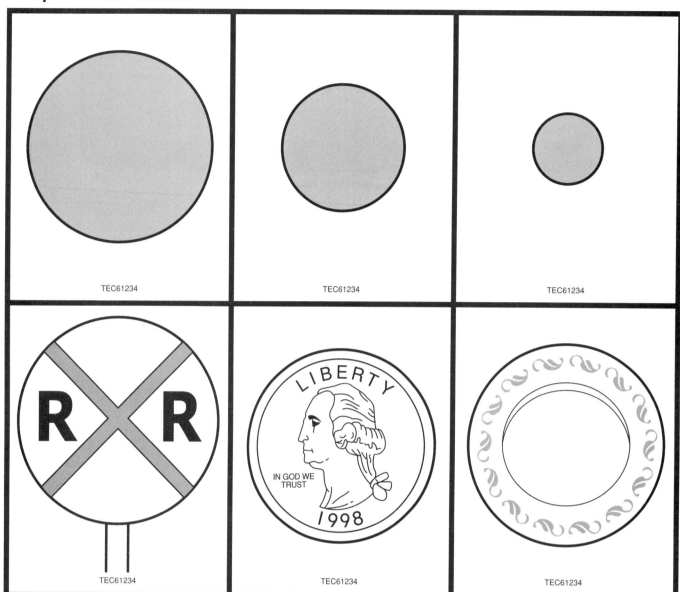

TEC61234

TEC61234

TEC61234

TEC61234

TEC61234

TEC61234

Distracter Cards

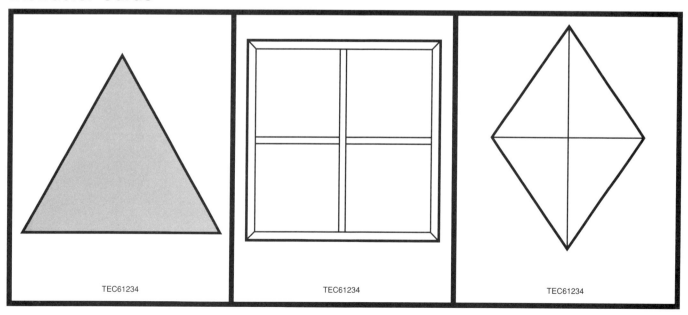

TEC61234

TEC61234

TEC61234

a clock,

A wheel,

and a button are

circles!

I Spy
Circles

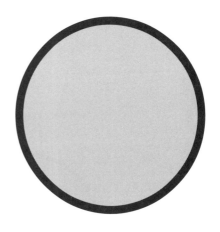

Name _____

Fold-and-Go Booklet: To make a booklet, cut on the bold booklet outline. Fold along the thin horizontal line (keeping the programming to the outside) and then fold along the thin vertical line (keeping the cover to the outside).

99

Name

100

Turtle Likes Circles

Trace.

Color.

Everything Colors & Shapes • ©The Mailbox® Books • TEC61234

Note to the teacher: Ask the child what shapes are on Turtle's shell. Then have the child trace and color each circle.

Name

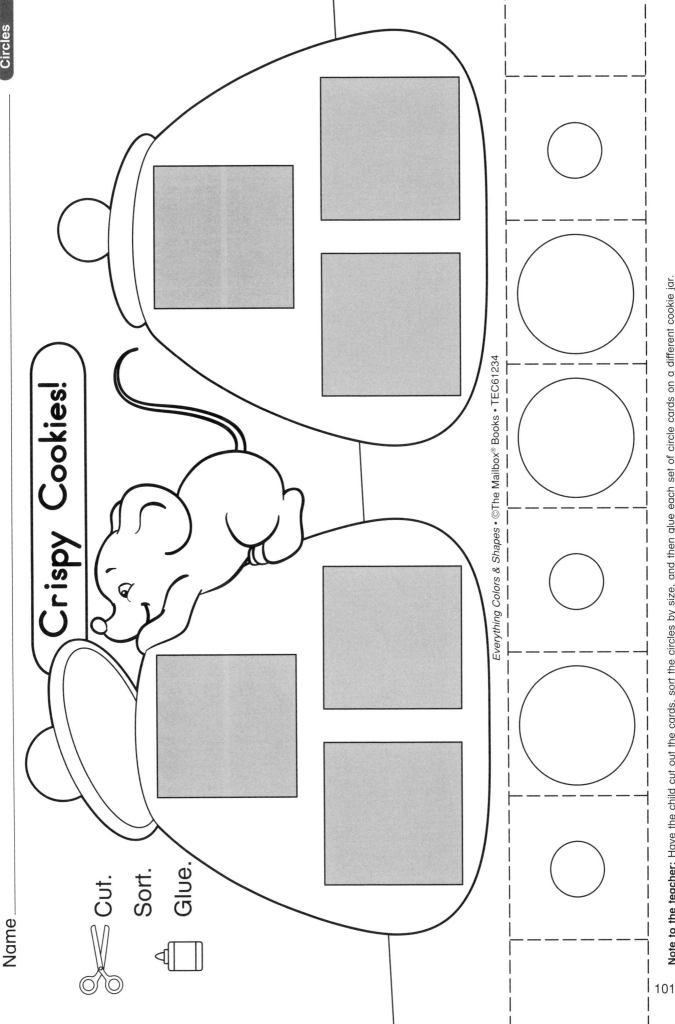

Crispy Cookies!

Cut.

Sort.

Glue.

Everything Colors & Shapes • ©The Mailbox® Books • TEC61234

Note to the teacher: Have the child cut out the cards, sort the circles by size, and then glue each set of circle cards on a different cookie jar.

Quick Craft

Hippo Stays Dry!

Materials: blue construction paper scraps, crayons or markers, glue

Directions: Draw and color circles on the umbrella. Then color the hippo and the puddle. Tear small pieces of construction paper and glue the pieces to the paper so they resemble raindrops.

Everything Colors & Shapes • ©The Mailbox® Books • TEC61234

square

Shape Cards: Squares

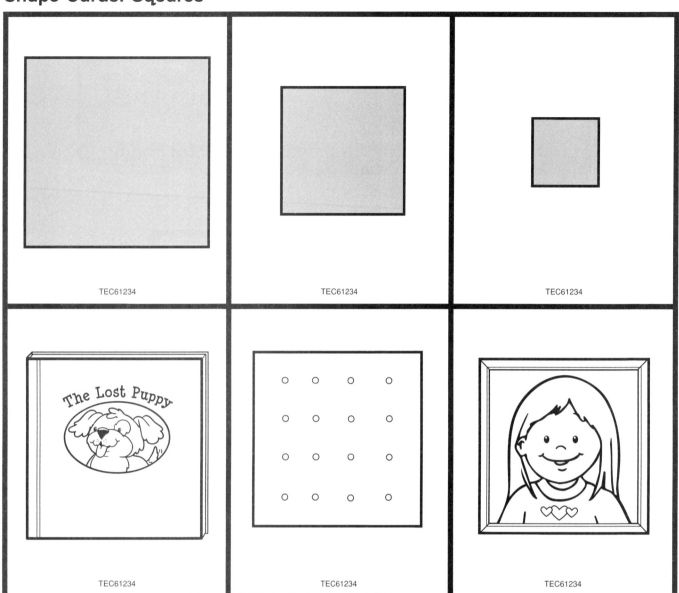

TEC61234

TEC61234

TEC61234

TEC61234

TEC61234

TEC61234

Distracter Cards

TEC61234

TEC61234

TEC61234

Everything Colors & Shapes • ©The Mailbox® Books • TEC61234

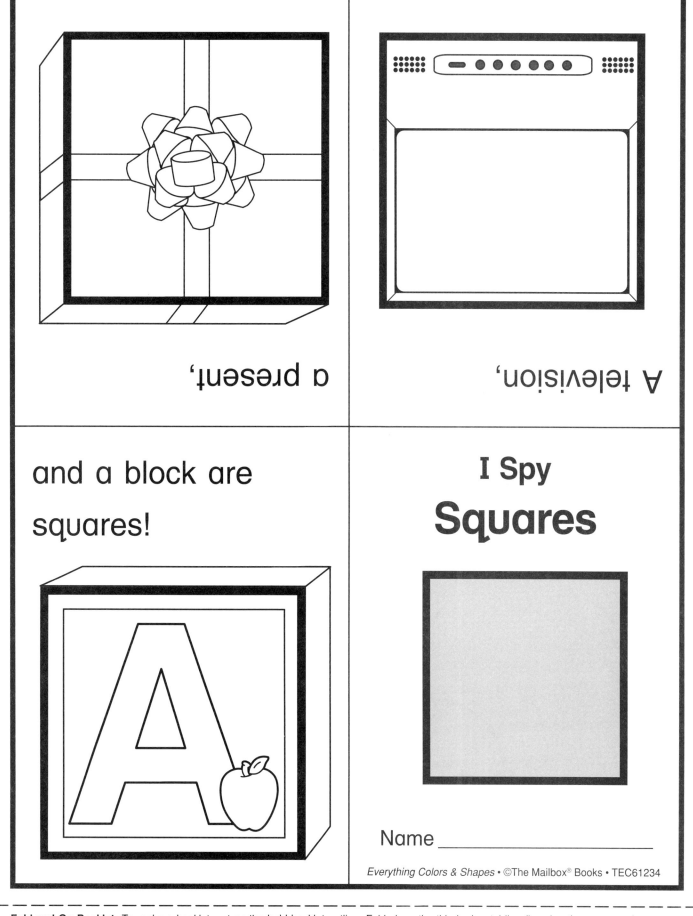

a present,

A television,

and a block are squares!

I Spy
Squares

Name _____

Fold-and-Go Booklet: To make a booklet, cut on the bold booklet outline. Fold along the thin horizontal line (keeping the programming to the outside) and then fold along the thin vertical line (keeping the cover to the outside).

105

Name

106

Turtle Likes Squares

Trace.

Color.

Everything Colors & Shapes • ©The Mailbox® Books • TEC61234

Note to the teacher: Ask the child what shapes are on the turtle's shell. Then have the child trace and color each square.

Name

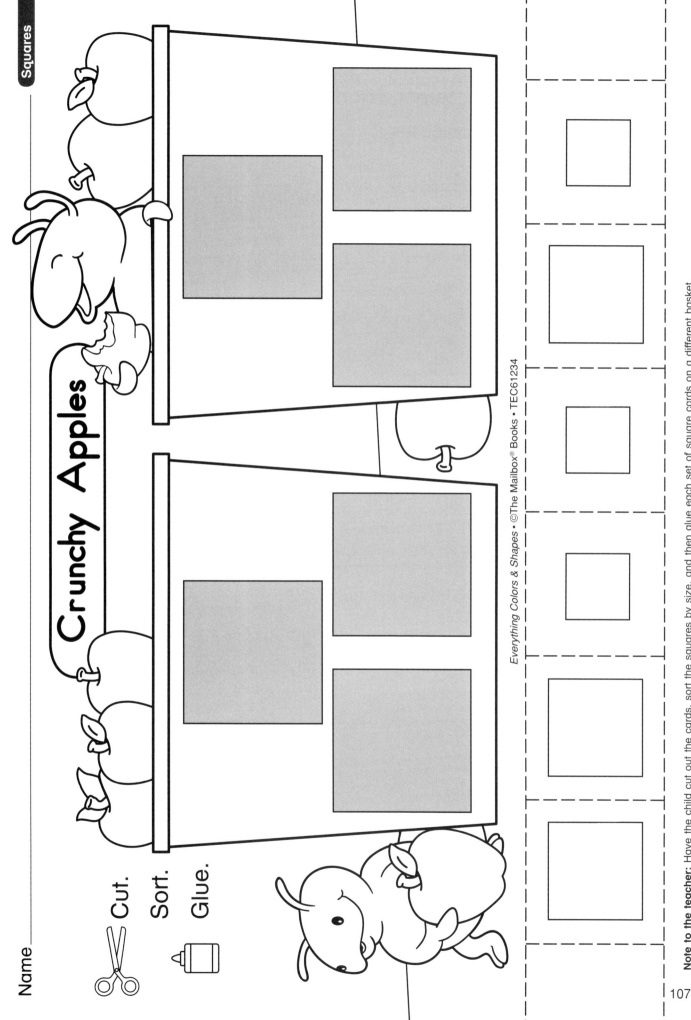

Squares

Crunchy Apples

Cut.
Sort.
Glue.

Everything Colors & Shapes • ©The Mailbox® Books • TEC61234

Note to the teacher: Have the child cut out the cards, sort the squares by size, and then glue each set of square cards on a different basket.

107

Quick Craft

Super Sand Castle

Materials: sand, crayons, glue

Directions: Draw squares to complete the sand castle. Then color the picture. Spread a thin layer of glue on the sand castle; then sprinkle sand on the glue.

Everything Colors & Shapes • ©The Mailbox® Books • TEC61234

triangle

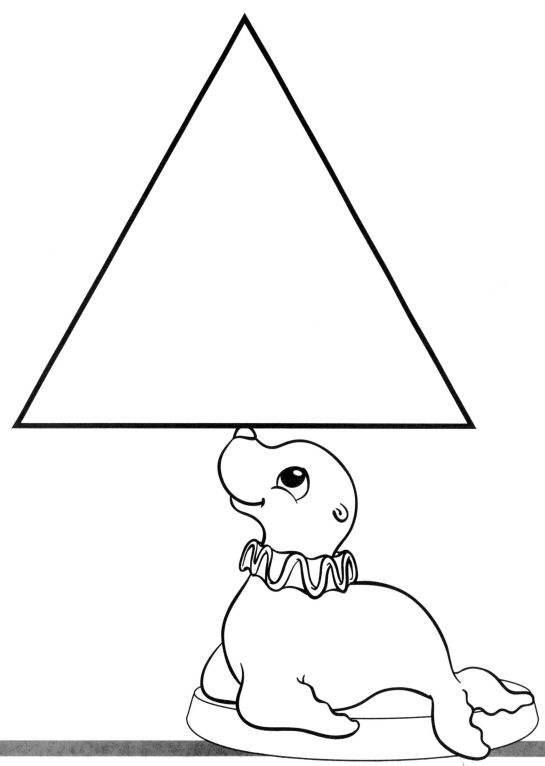

Shape Cards: Triangles

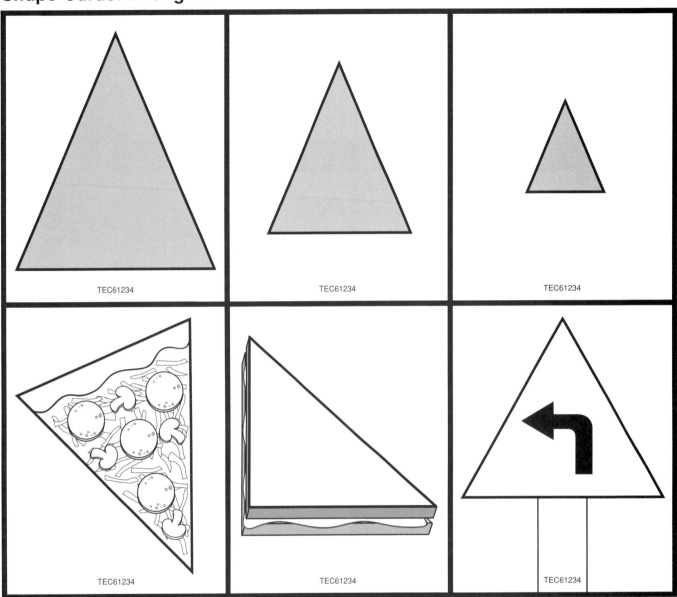

TEC61234

TEC61234

TEC61234

TEC61234

TEC61234

TEC61234

Distracter Cards

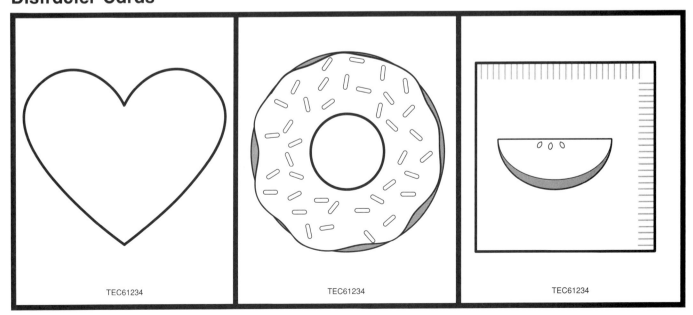

TEC61234

TEC61234

TEC61234

Everything Colors & Shapes • ©The Mailbox® Books • TEC61234

a pizza slice,

A boat sail,

and a flag are
triangles!

I Spy
Triangles

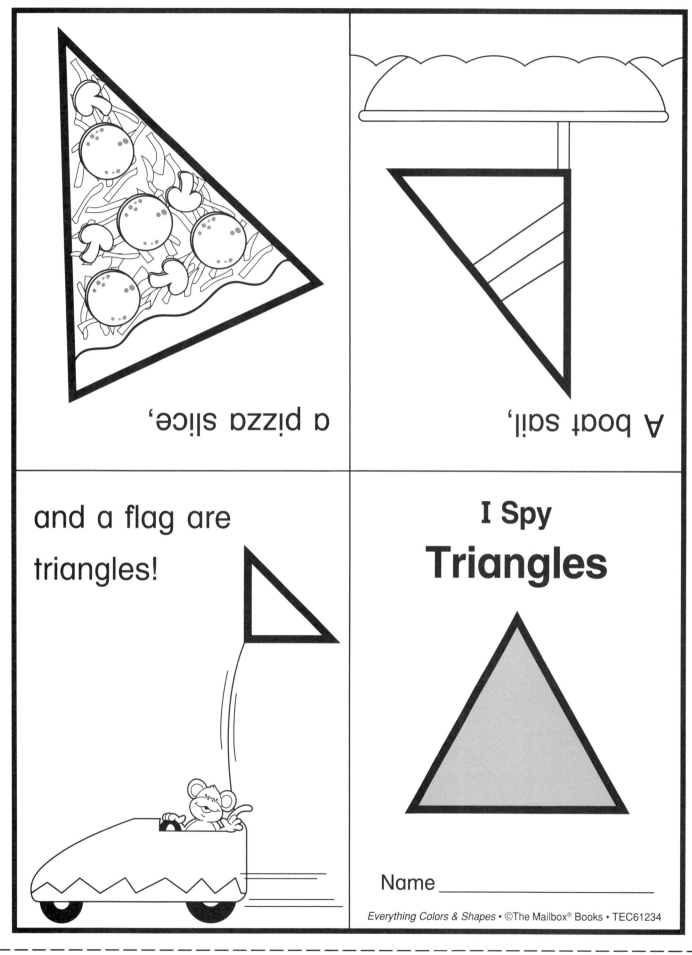

Name _____

Everything Colors & Shapes • ©The Mailbox® Books • TEC61234

Fold-and-Go Booklet: To make a booklet, cut on the bold booklet outline. Fold along the thin horizontal line (keeping the programming to the outside) and then fold along the thin vertical line (keeping the cover to the outside).

111

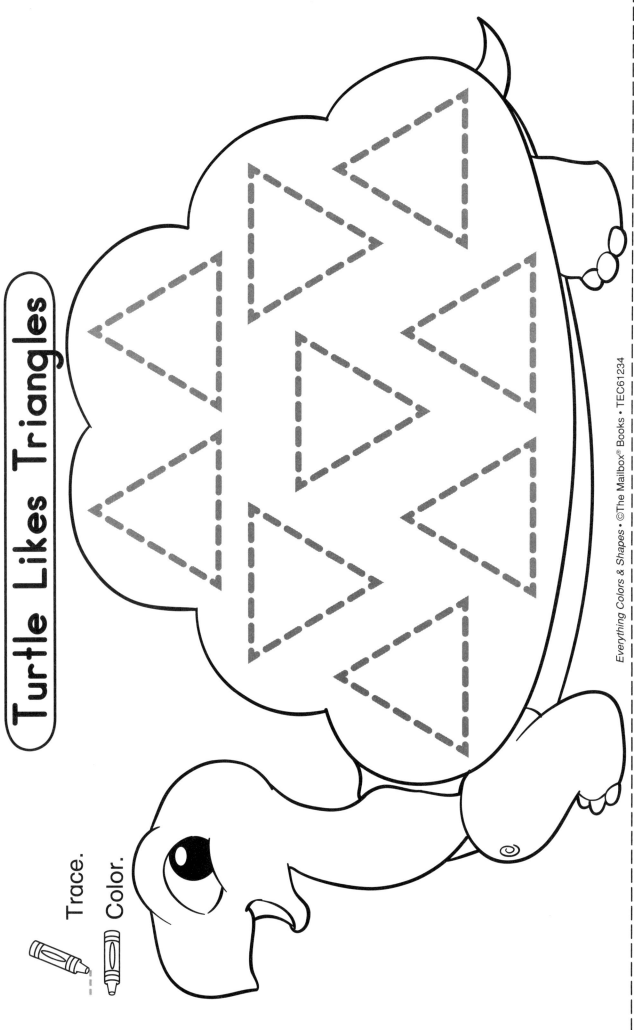

Name _____

Turtle Likes Triangles

Trace.

Color.

Everything Colors & Shapes • ©The Mailbox® Books • TEC61234

112

Note to the teacher: Ask the child what shapes are on the turtle's shell. Then have the child trace and color each triangle.

Name _____

Yummy Honey

Cut.

Sort.

Glue.

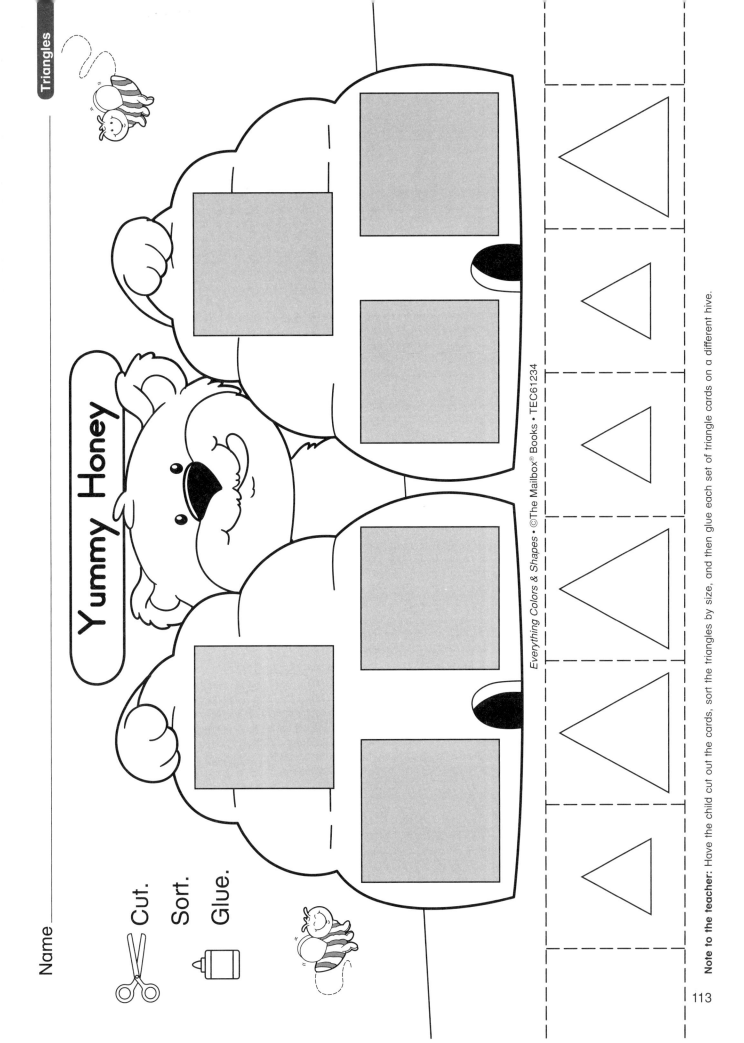

Everything Colors & Shapes • ©The Mailbox® Books • TEC61234

Note to the teacher: Have the child cut out the cards, sort the triangles by size, and then glue each set of triangle cards on a different hive.

113

Fly, Dragon, Fly!

Materials: cotton batting (or cotton balls), crayons or markers, glue

Directions: Draw and color triangular scales along the upper edge of the dragon, from its head to the tip of its tail. Then color the rest of the dragon and the sky. Spread glue on the cloud shape. Press cotton batting on the glue.

rectangle

Shape Cards: Rectangles

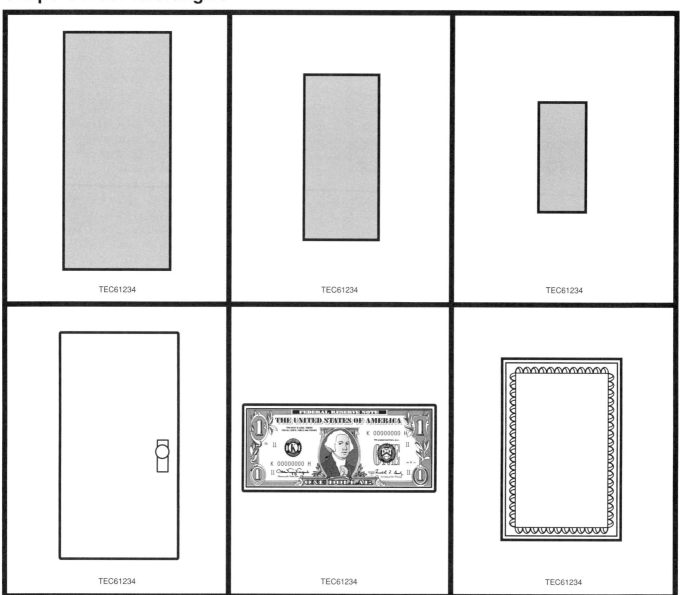

TEC61234

TEC61234

TEC61234

TEC61234

TEC61234

TEC61234

Distracter Cards

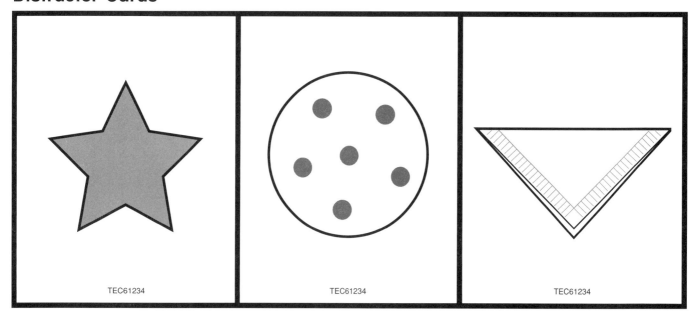

TEC61234

TEC61234

TEC61234

Everything Colors & Shapes • ©The Mailbox® Books • TEC61234

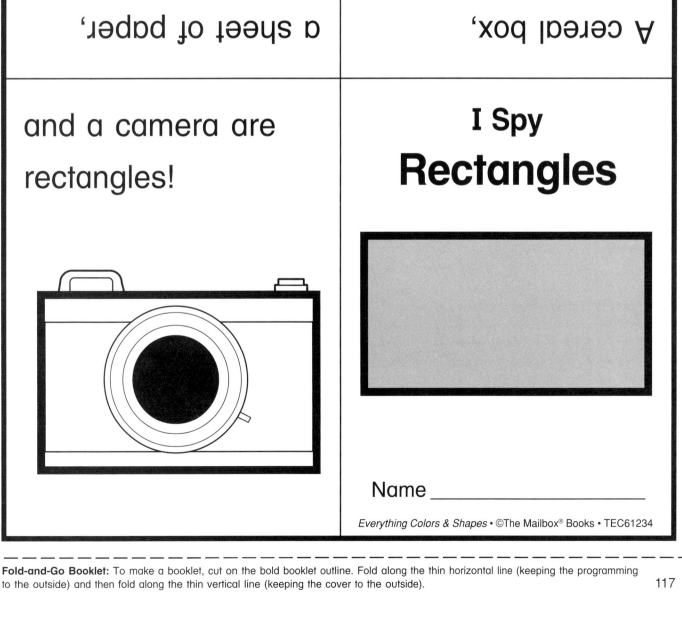

a sheet of paper,

A cereal box,

and a camera are rectangles!

I Spy
Rectangles

Name _____

Fold-and-Go Booklet: To make a booklet, cut on the bold booklet outline. Fold along the thin horizontal line (keeping the programming to the outside) and then fold along the thin vertical line (keeping the cover to the outside).

Name

Turtle Likes Rectangles

Trace.

Color.

Everything Colors & Shapes • ©The Mailbox® Books • TEC61234

118

Note to the teacher: Ask the child what shapes are on the turtle's shell. Then have the child trace and color each rectangle.

Name

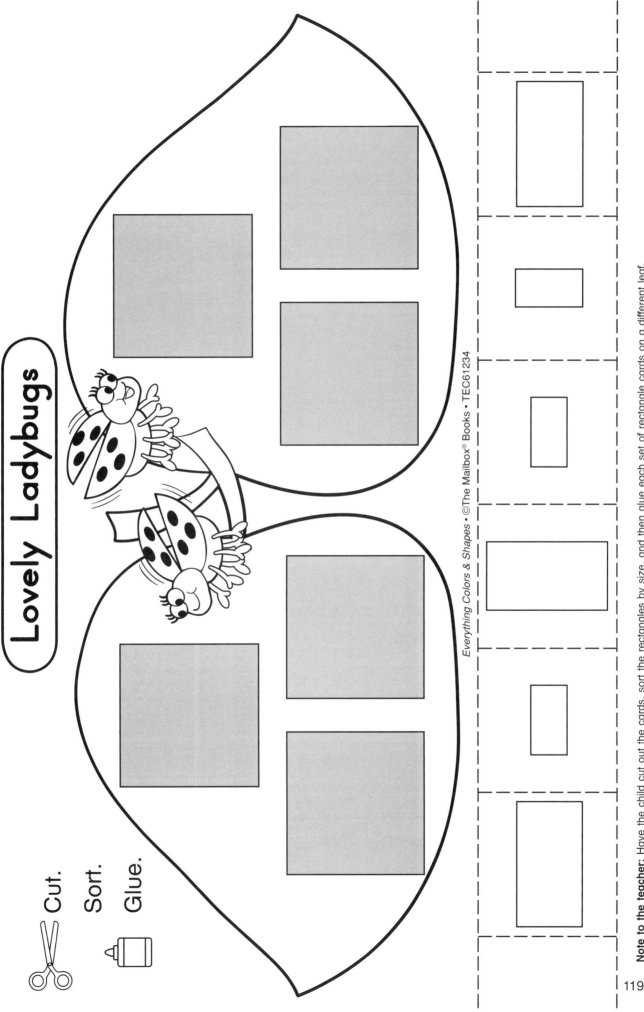

Lovely Ladybugs

Cut.

Sort.

Glue.

Everything Colors & Shapes • ©The Mailbox® Books • TEC61234

Note to the teacher: Have the child cut out the cards, sort the rectangles by size, and then glue each set of rectangle cards on a different leaf.

119

Quick Craft

Shiny School Bus

Materials: yellow tissue paper scraps, markers, glue

Directions: Draw rectangular windows on the bus above the black line; then draw a face in each window. Tear small pieces of tissue paper and glue them to the bus below the windows. To give the bus a shiny effect, spread a thin layer of glue over the tissue paper and allow it to dry.

Everything Colors & Shapes • ©The Mailbox® Books • TEC61234

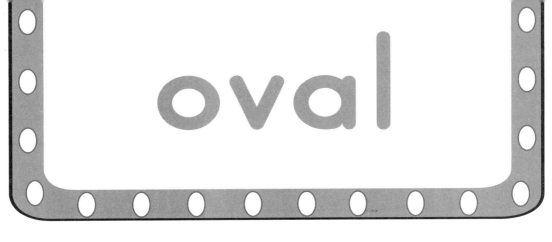

Shape Cards: Ovals

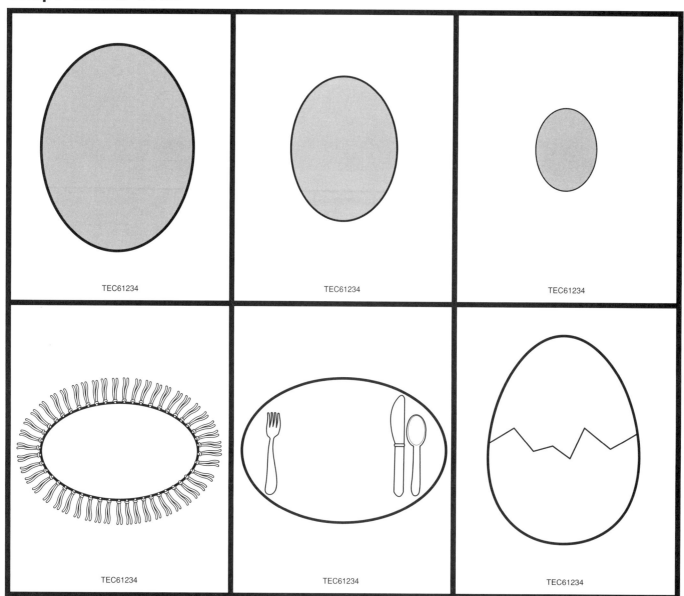

TEC61234

TEC61234

TEC61234

TEC61234

TEC61234

TEC61234

Distracter Cards

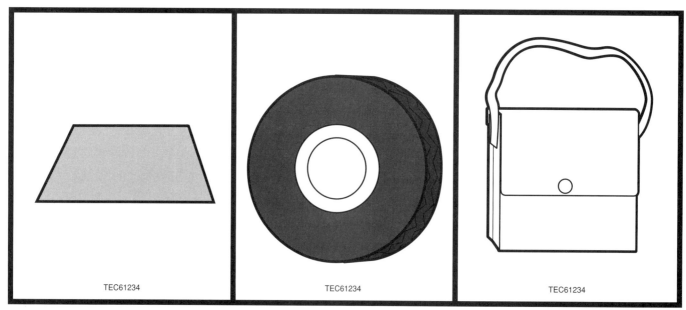

TEC61234

TEC61234

TEC61234

Everything Colors & Shapes • ©The Mailbox® Books • TEC61234

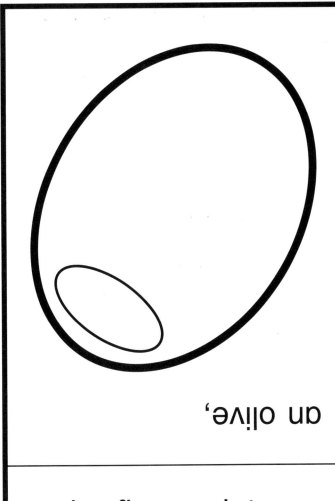

an olive,

A picture frame,

and a fingerprint are ovals!

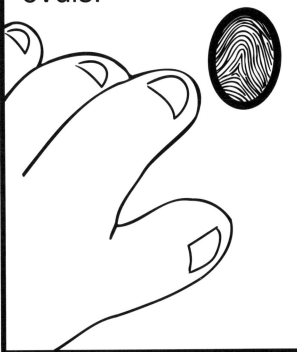

I Spy
Ovals

Name _____

Everything Colors & Shapes • ©The Mailbox® Books • TEC61234

Fold-and-Go Booklet: To make a booklet, cut on the bold booklet outline. Fold along the thin horizontal line (keeping the programming to the outside) and then fold along the thin vertical line (keeping the cover to the outside).

123

Name _____

Turtle Likes Ovals

Trace.

Color.

Everything Colors & Shapes • ©The Mailbox® Books • TEC61234

Note to the teacher: Ask the child what shapes are on the turtle's shell. Then have the child trace and color each oval.

Name

Groceries Galore!

Spinach

CRACKERS

Cut.

Sort.

Glue.

Everything Colors & Shapes • ©The Mailbox® Books • TEC61234

Note to the teacher: Have the child cut out the cards, sort the ovals by size, and then glue each set of oval cards on a different bag.

Quick Craft

Gathering Eggs!

Materials: brown crinkle strips, crayons or markers, glue

Directions: Draw oval-shaped eggs along the straw line; then color the hen and basket. Spread glue in small sections on the bottom of the paper; then press crinkle strips on the glue so they resemble straw.

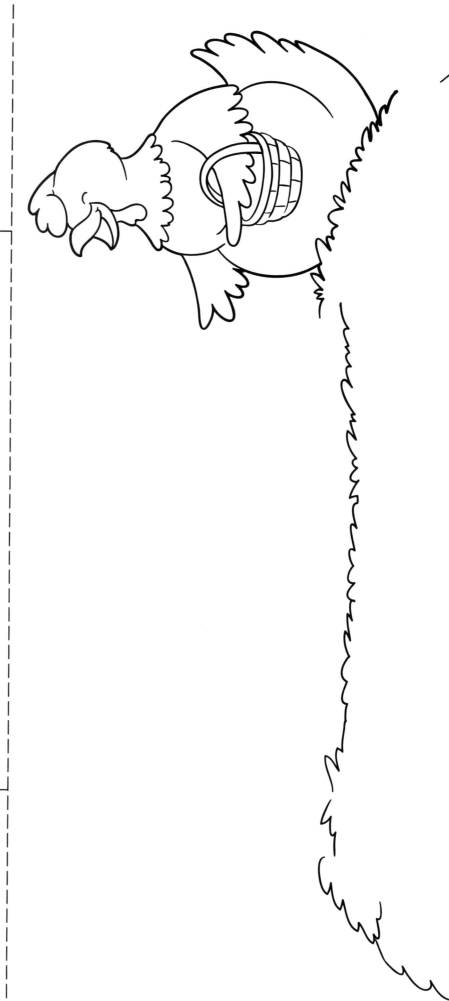

Everything Colors & Shapes • ©The Mailbox® Books • TEC61234

star

Shape Cards: Stars

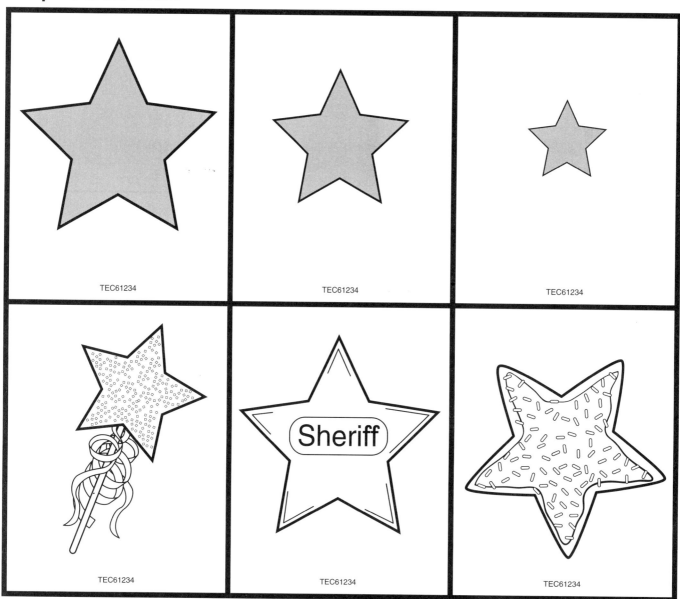

TEC61234

TEC61234

TEC61234

TEC61234

TEC61234

TEC61234

Distracter Cards

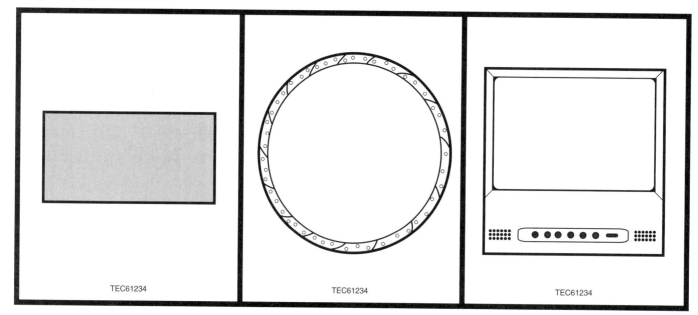

TEC61234

TEC61234

TEC61234

a magic wand,

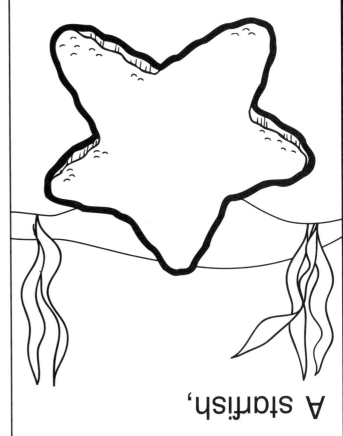

A starfish,

and sprinkles are
stars!

I Spy
Stars

Name _____

Fold-and-Go Booklet: To make a booklet, cut on the bold booklet outline. Fold along the thin horizontal line (keeping the programming to the outside) and then fold along the thin vertical line (keeping the cover to the outside).

Name

130

Turtle Likes Stars

Trace.

Color.

Everything Colors & Shapes • ©The Mailbox® Books • TEC61234

Note to the teacher: Ask the child what shapes are on the turtle's shell. Then have the child trace and color each star.

Name

Birthday Surprise!

Cut.

Sort.

Glue.

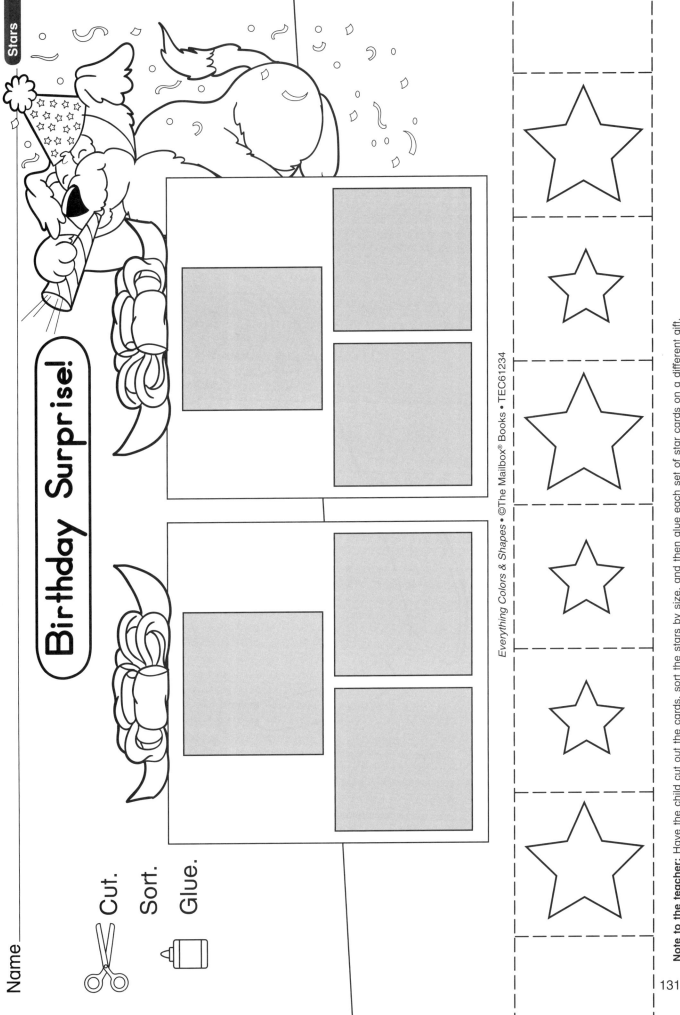

Everything Colors & Shapes • ©The Mailbox® Books • TEC61234

Note to the teacher: Have the child cut out the cards, sort the stars by size, and then glue each set of star cards on a different gift.

Stars

Quick Craft

Blast Off!

Materials: aluminum foil squares, cotton batting, crayons or markers, glue

Directions: Draw and color stars around the rocket; then color the sky black. Tear aluminum foil and glue the pieces to the rocket, leaving the window uncovered. Then glue cotton batting to the bottom of the rocket.

Everything Colors & Shapes • ©The Mailbox® Books • TEC61234

heart

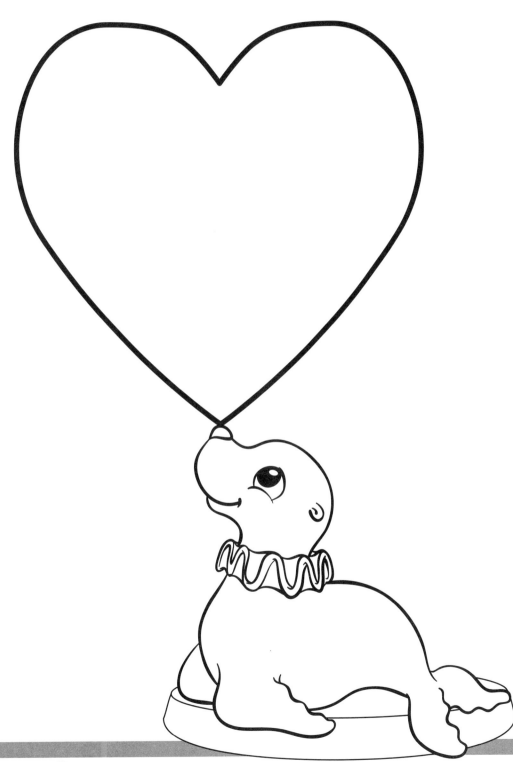

Shape Cards: Hearts

TEC61234

TEC61234

TEC61234

TEC61234

TEC61234

TEC61234

Distracter Cards

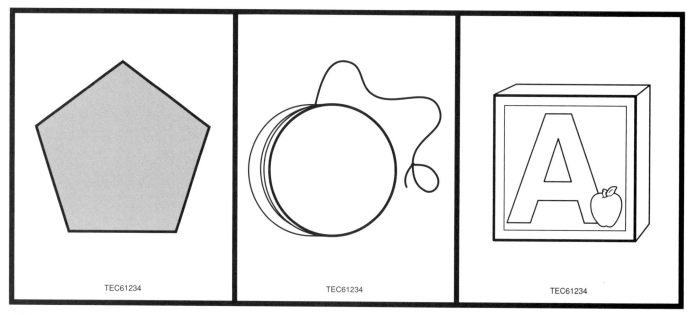

TEC61234

TEC61234

TEC61234

Everything Colors & Shapes • ©The Mailbox® Books • TEC61234

You are
Sweet!

a piece of candy,

I love
you!

A balloon,

and a cookie are
hearts!

I Spy
Hearts

Name _____

Fold-and-Go Booklet: To make a booklet, cut on the bold booklet outline. Fold along the thin horizontal line (keeping the programming to the outside) and then fold along the thin vertical line (keeping the cover to the outside).

Name

136

Turtle Likes Hearts

Trace.

Color.

Everything Colors & Shapes • ©The Mailbox® Books • TEC61234

Note to the teacher: Ask the child what shapes are on the turtle's shell. Then have the child trace and color each heart.

Name

Building Castles

✂ Cut.

Sort.

Glue.

Everything Colors & Shapes • ©The Mailbox® Books • TEC61234

Note to the teacher: Have the child cut out the cards, sort the hearts by size, and then glue each set of heart cards on a different sand castle.

137

A Tasty Cake!

Materials: several containers of lightly tinted glue, sprinkles, small tissue paper squares, markers, glue

Directions: Draw several heart shapes on the cake. Paint each heart with tinted glue; then press sprinkles on the glue. Glue crumpled tissue paper squares to the top of the cake to create flower decorations.

diamond

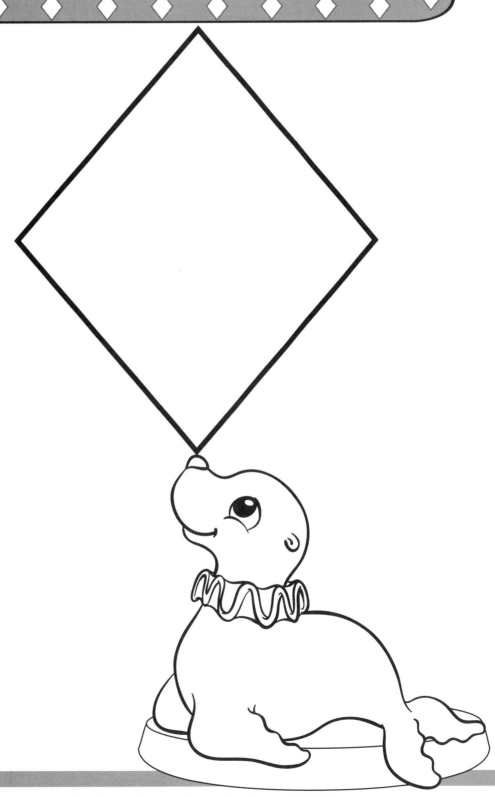

Shape Cards: Diamonds

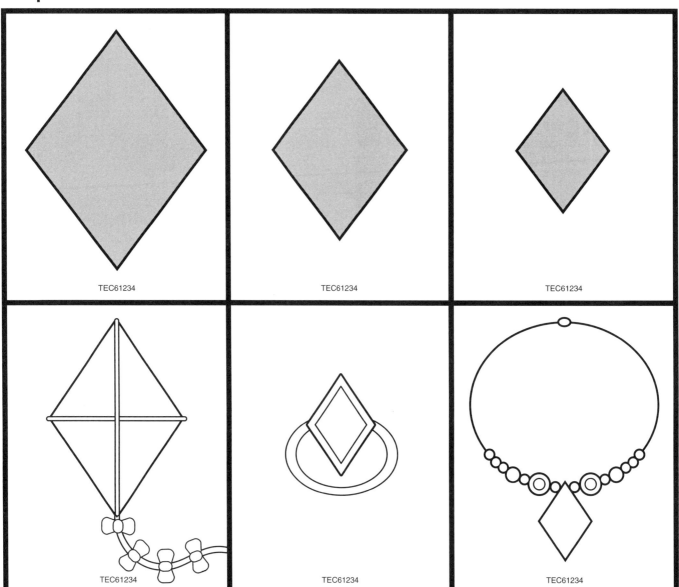

TEC61234

TEC61234

TEC61234

TEC61234

TEC61234

TEC61234

Distracter Cards

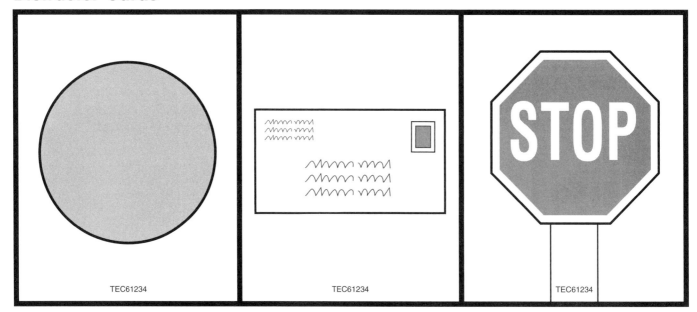

TEC61234

TEC61234

TEC61234

Everything Colors & Shapes • ©The Mailbox® Books • TEC61234

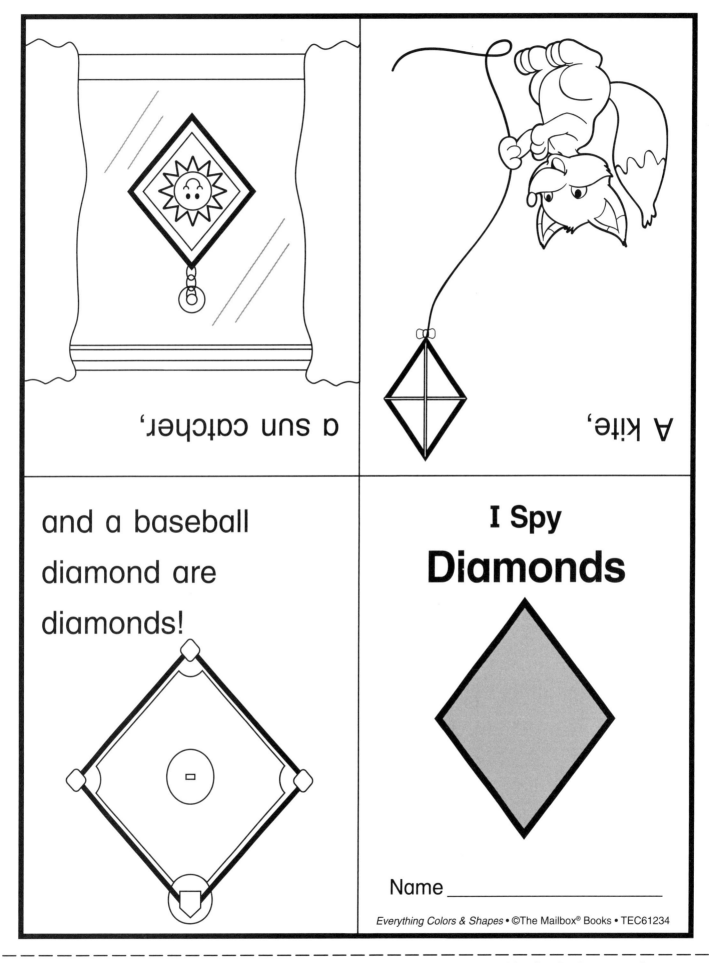

a sun catcher,

A kite,

and a baseball diamond are diamonds!

I Spy
Diamonds

Name _____

Everything Colors & Shapes • ©The Mailbox® Books • TEC61234

Fold-and-Go Booklet: To make a booklet, cut on the bold booklet outline. Fold along the thin horizontal line (keeping the programming to the outside) and then fold along the thin vertical line (keeping the cover to the outside).

141

Name

Turtle Likes Diamonds

Trace.

Color.

Everything Colors & Shapes • ©The Mailbox® Books • TEC61234

Note to the teacher: Ask the child what shapes are on the turtle's shell. Then have the child trace and color each diamond.

Name

Cut.

Sort.

Glue.

Thirsty Bees

Everything Colors & Shapes • ©The Mailbox® Books • TEC61234

Note to the teacher: Have the child cut out the cards, sort the diamonds by size, and then glue each set of diamond cards on a different glass.

143

Quick Craft

Flying High!

Materials: yarn, squeeze bottle of glue, crayons or markers

Directions: Draw diamond-shaped kites at the top of each kite string. Then color the kites. Squeeze glue along each kite string and then press a length of yarn on the glue.

Everything Colors & Shapes • ©The Mailbox® Books • TEC61234

Shape-O Game

Pages 145 and 146

To prepare, make one copy of the gameboard on page 146 and give each child a copy of a game strip from below. Players also need crayons and a pom-pom.

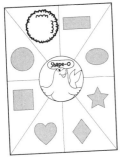
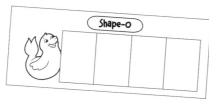

To play, have players alternate tossing the pom-pom onto the gameboard. A player names the shape in the game space where the pom-pom lands. (When the pom-pom lands in the center circle, he may point to and name any shape on the gameboard.) Then the player draws and colors the shape in a blank box on his game strip. Continue play until each player fills his game strip or until game time is over.

For an alternate version, specify that shapes may not be repeated on a player's game strip. When a player rolls a shape he has already drawn on his game strip, he names the shape and his turn is over. The first player with four different shapes on his game strip wins.

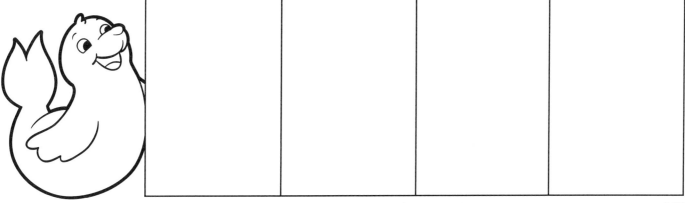

Note to the teacher: Use this gameboard with the directions on page 145.

Shape Cards

Pages 147–152

Preparing and using the cards:

Make one construction paper copy of the cards on pages 148–151. Cut out the cards and use them as desired. Possible activities include

- **Shape recognition:** Name a shape and ask a child to find a matching shape card.

- **Shape identification:** Ask a child to point to each of several shape cards and name the shape that is shown.

- **Shape awareness:** Give a child a shape card. Ask the child to locate another object in the room that has a similar shape, such as a clock or a button for a circle, a sticker or a star-shaped pointer for a star, and a book or a carpet square for a rectangle.

- **Sorting:** Sort by shape, size, straight lines, curved lines, corners, curved edges, or straight edges.

- **Seriation:** Arrange matching shapes from smallest to largest.

Make two construction paper copies of the cards on pages 148–151, cut out the cards, and use them for **shape matching** and to play a variety of **memory games.**

Program the blank cards on page 152 with additional shapes.

Everything Colors & Shapes • ©The Mailbox® Books • TEC61234

147

Shape Cards

Use with the directions on page 147.

TEC61234

TEC61234

TEC61234

TEC61234

TEC61234

TEC61234

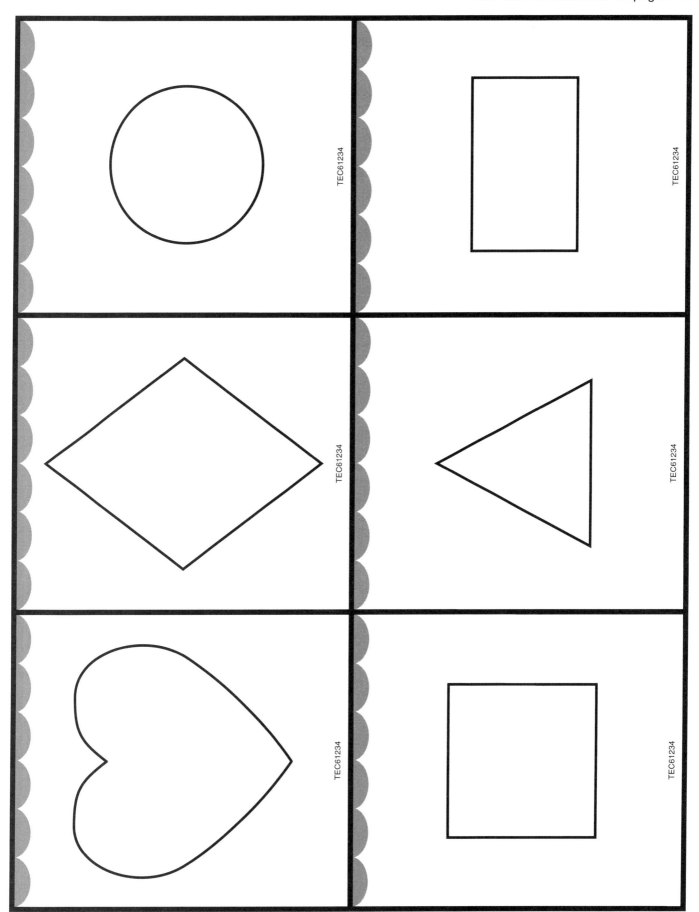

TEC61234

TEC61234

TEC61234

TEC61234

TEC61234

TEC61234

Shape Cards
Use with the directions on page 147.

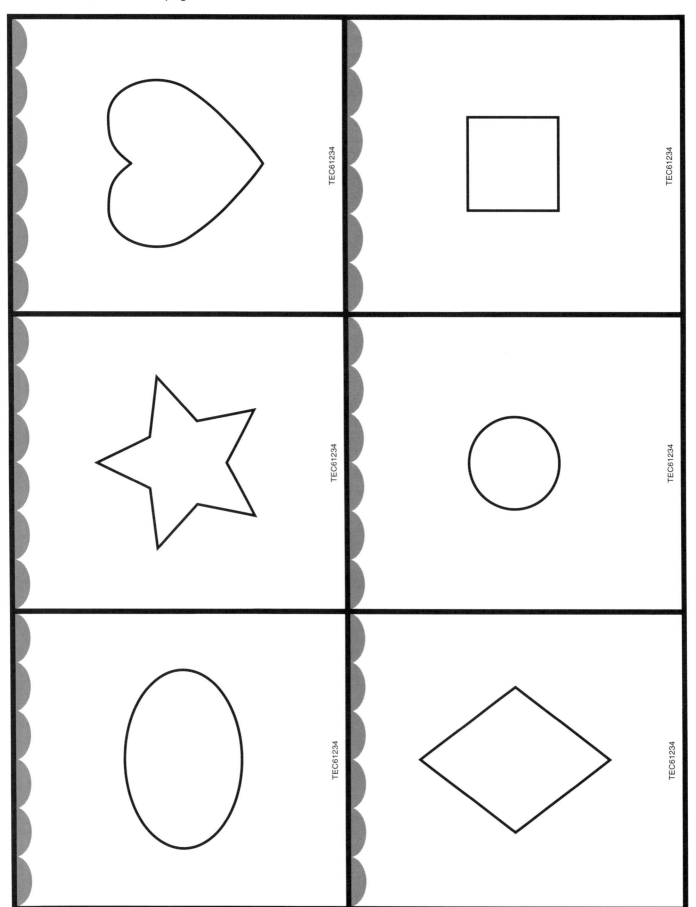

TEC61234

TEC61234

TEC61234

TEC61234

TEC61234

TEC61234

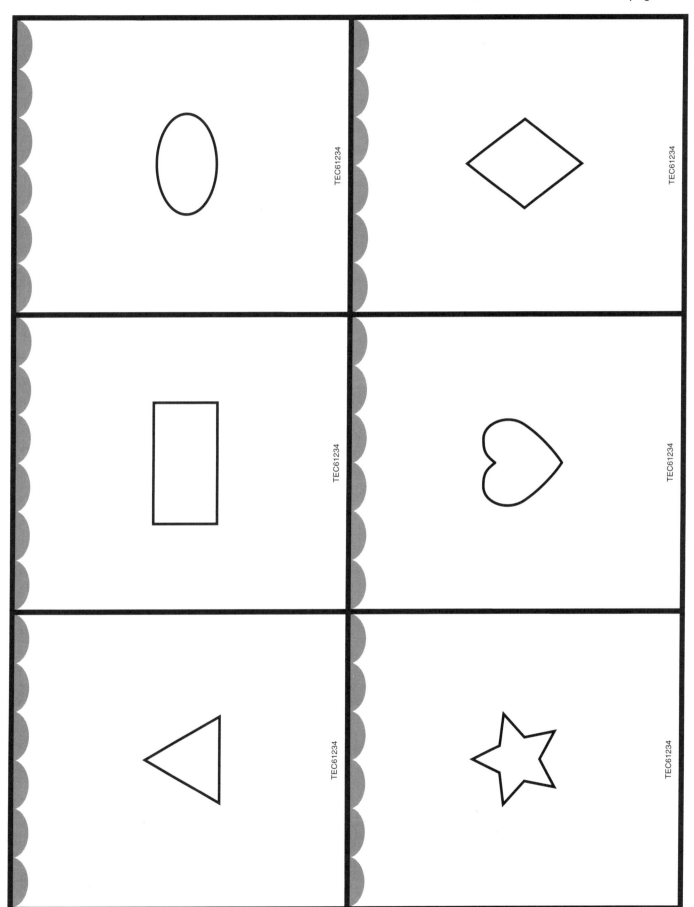

TEC61234

TEC61234

TEC61234

TEC61234

TEC61234

TEC61234

Blank Cards

Program the cards with additional shapes or use as desired.

TEC61234

TEC61234

TEC61234

TEC61234

TEC61234

TEC61234

Booklet-Making Activity

Pages 153–158

Preparing a booklet:

1. Copy pages 154–158 on white paper.
2. Cut apart the booklet cover and pages.
3. Stack the shape pages atop the review page and put the booklet cover on top.
4. Staple the left edge of the booklet.

Completing a booklet:

1. Help a child write her name on the booklet cover. Then have her color the artwork.
2. Read aloud the shape name on each shape page and verify that the child can identify the shape. Then read aloud the instruction. Ask the child to color each shape she finds. Provide assistance as needed in finding any remaining shapes.

Name_____

Shapes on the Farm

Everything Colors & Shapes • ©The Mailbox® Books • TEC61234

Find 6.

circles

154 **Booklet Cover and Shape Page:** Use with the directions on page 153.

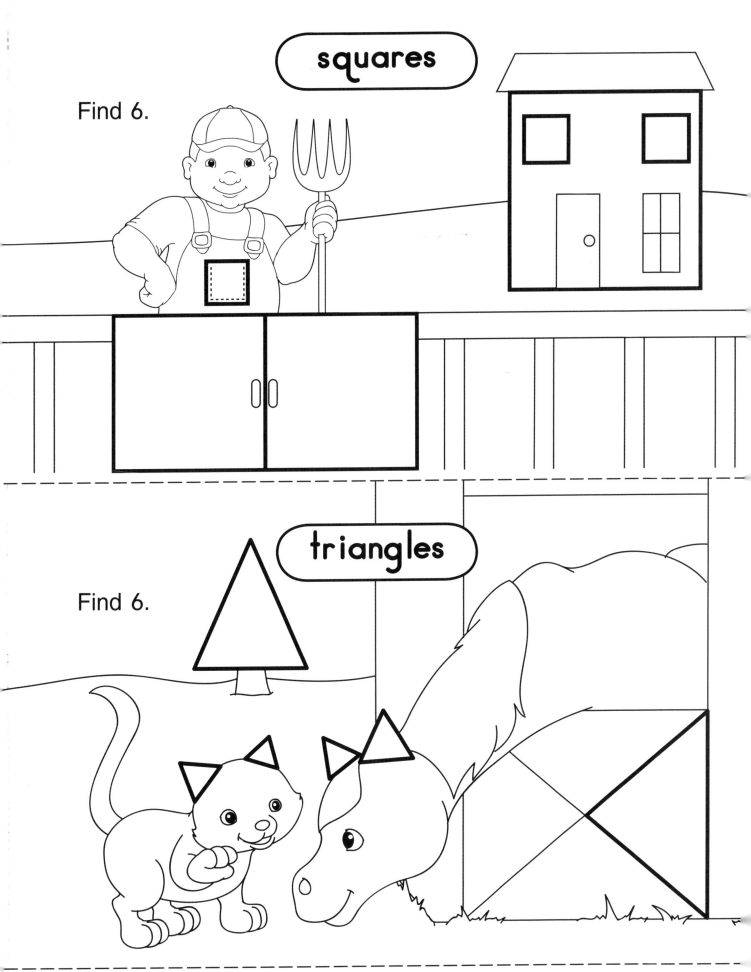

squares

Find 6.

triangles

Find 6.

Booklet Shape Pages: Use with the directions on page 153.

rectangles

Find 6.

ovals

Find 6.

Everything Colors & Shapes • ©The Mailbox® Books • TEC61234

156 **Booklet Shape Pages:** Use with the directions on page 153.

stars

Find 6.

hearts

Find 6.

Everything Colors & Shapes • ©The Mailbox® Books • TEC61234

Booklet Shape Pages: Use with the directions on page 153.

157

diamonds

Find 6.

Can you find 1 of each shape?

Name_____

Two of a Kind

Color.

Note to the teacher: Have the student color the two shapes in each row that match.

Name _____

Color.

Duck's Doughnuts

 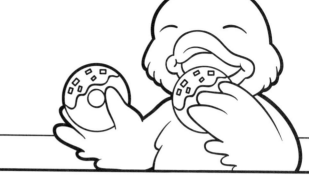

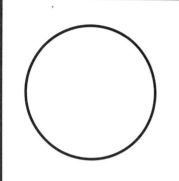  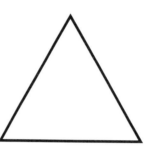 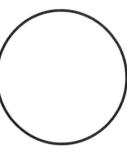

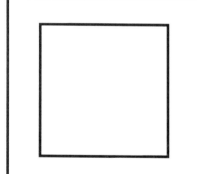   

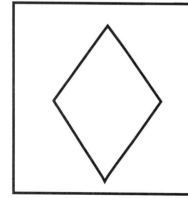  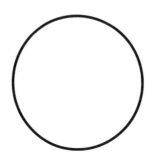 

Everything Colors & Shapes • ©The Mailbox® Books • TEC61234

160   **Note to the teacher:** Have the student color the two shapes in each row that match.

Name_____

Bath Time!

Color.

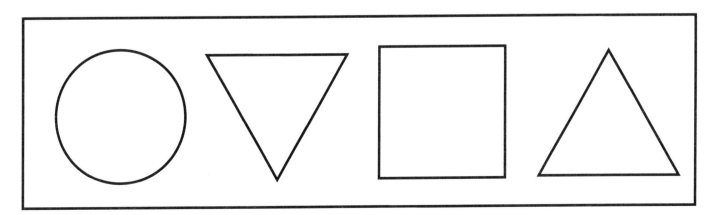

Note to the teacher: Have the student color the two shapes in each row that match.

Name _____

Shapes

Sandy Shapes

Color each ☐.
Find 8 in all.

162   *Everything Colors & Shapes* • ©The Mailbox® Books • TEC61234

Name

Bear's Bedroom

🖍 Color each ☐.

Find 6 in all.

Everything Colors & Shapes • ©The Mailbox® Books • TEC61234

Name _____

164

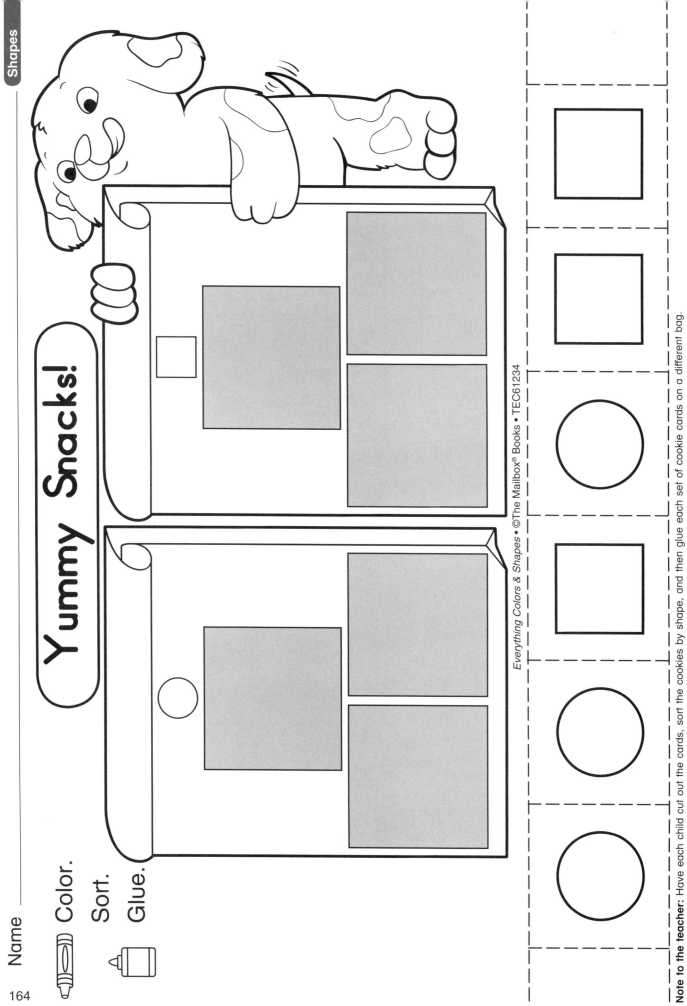

Yummy Snacks!

Color.

Sort.

Glue.

Everything Colors & Shapes • ©The Mailbox® Books • TEC61234

Note to the teacher: Have each child cut out the cards, sort the cookies by shape, and then glue each set of cookie cards on a different bag.

Name _____

All Cleaned Up!

 Color.

Sort.

Glue.

Everything Colors & Shapes • ©The Mailbox® Books • TEC61234

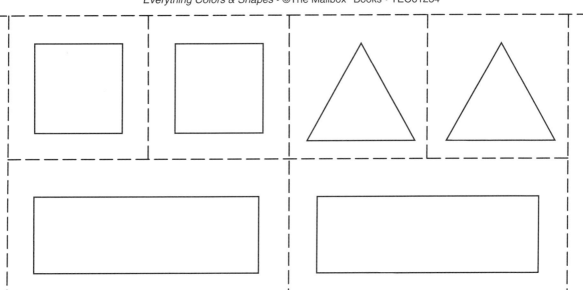

Note to the teacher: Have the child cut out the cards, sort the blocks by shape, and then glue each set of block cards on a different shelf.

Name

Matching Mittens

✂ Cut.

🖊 Glue to make matching pairs.

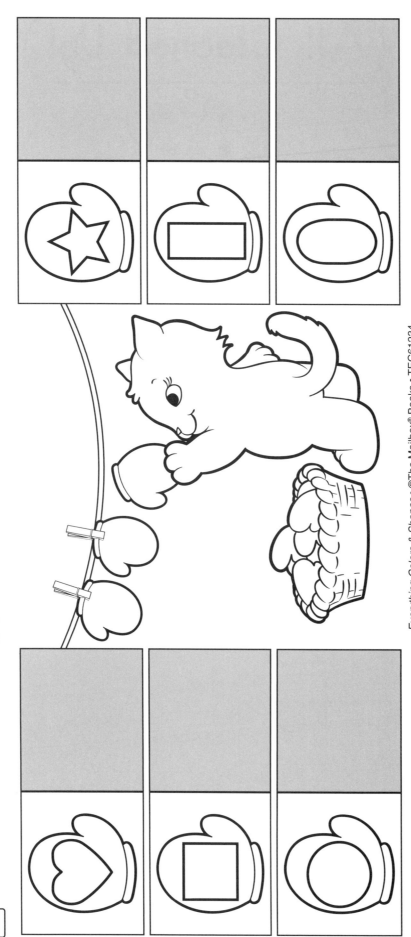

Everything Colors & Shapes • ©The Mailbox® Books • TEC61234

166

Name

Trace.

Fox Family Photos

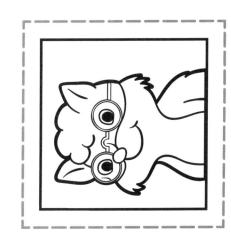

Everything Colors & Shapes • ©The Mailbox® Books • TEC61234

167

Name_____

Crispy Crackers!

Trace.

Draw.

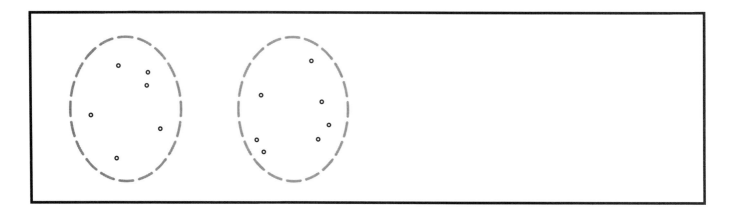

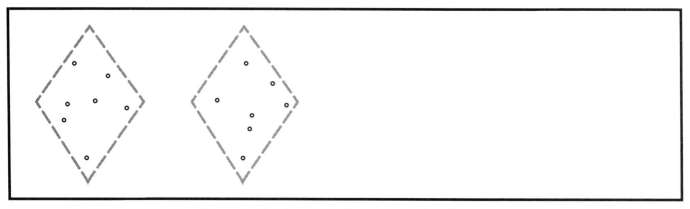

Everything Colors & Shapes • ©The Mailbox® Books • TEC61234

Note to the teacher: Have the student trace the shapes in each row; then have him draw the shape in the space provided.

Name_____

Sewing Buttons

Trace.

Draw.

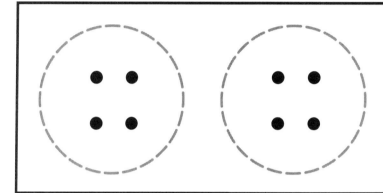

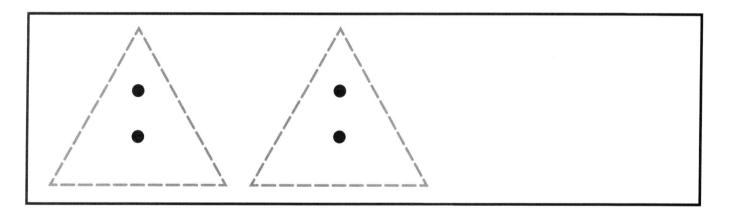

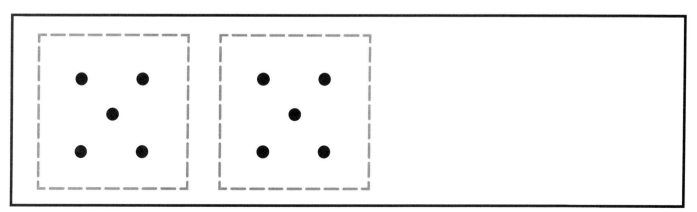

Note to the teacher: Have the student trace the shapes in each row; then have her draw the shape in the space provided.

Name _____

Hippo Goes Camping

Color.

Color Code

◯ —red   △ —yellow

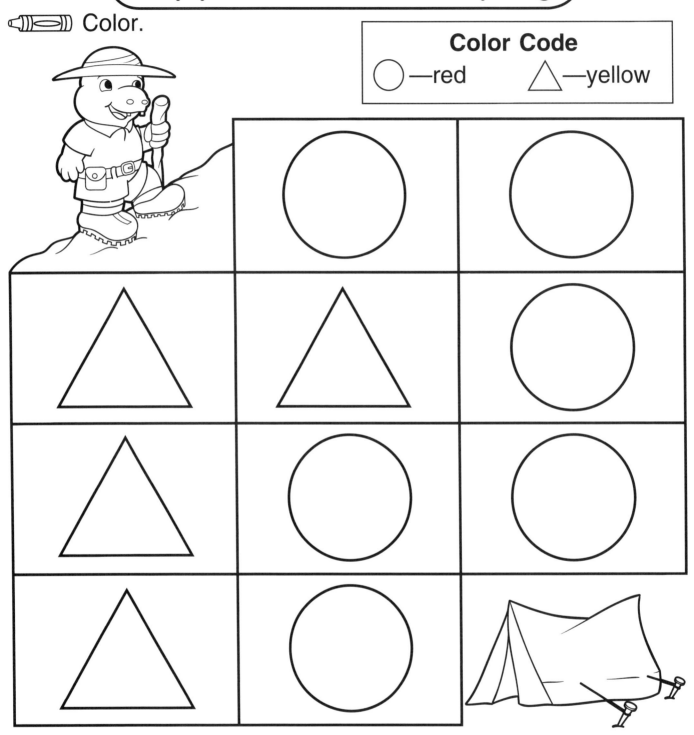

Color the shape that makes a path to Hippo's tent.

Everything Colors & Shapes • ©The Mailbox® Books • TEC61234

Note to the teacher: Have the student color each shape in the color code; then have him use the code to color the shape in each box.

Name

Showtime!

Listen and do.

Everything Colors & Shapes • ©The Mailbox® Books • TEC61234

Note to the teacher: Have the student color each set of shapes a different color.

Full-Size Shape Page

Center: Laminate a copy of a shape page and place it at a center along with play dough, plastic knives, and shape cookie cutters. A youngster makes matching shapes from play dough and places them on the mat. **Shape matching**

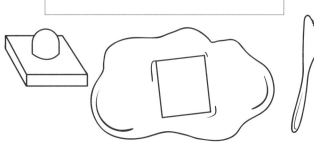

Large group: Show the group a shape page. Have each child draw the shape on an individual whiteboard. After assessing each child's shape, have her wipe off her board; then show her a different shape page. **Drawing shapes**

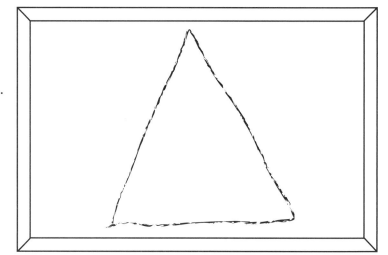

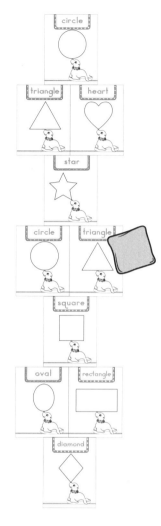

Small group: Use clear Con-Tact covering to attach several different shape pages to the floor in an open area in a hopscotch pattern. A child tosses a beanbag at the first shape. Then he hops on the shape and says its name. He continues tossing, hopping, and naming shapes until he has named each shape in order. **Shape identification**

Shape and Distracter Cards

Center: Copy and cut out a set of cards and one distracter card. A child lays the cards facedown on a table. She turns over one card at a time, trying to turn over all six shape cards before turning over the distracter card. If she turns over the distracter card, she turns all the cards facedown again, mixes them, and starts over. **Shape matching**

Shape and Distracter Cards

Large group: Secretly hide the cards for three or four shapes around the room. (Set aside the distracter cards.) Label a card for each shape and place each card in a separate row of a pocket chart. Invite youngsters to search for the shape cards. When a child finds a card, he places it in the corresponding row of the pocket chart. **Shape sorting**

Center: Stack one each of several different shape cards facedown at a center. A child chooses a card and draws the shape as many times as she can on a sheet of paper. Then she turns the paper over and repeats the process with a different shape card. **Drawing shapes**

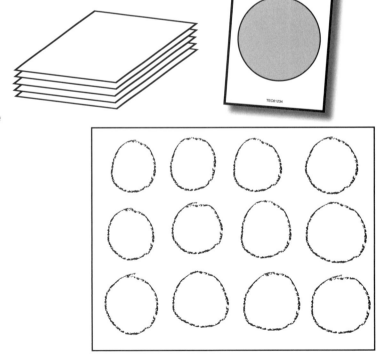

Fold-and-Go Booklet

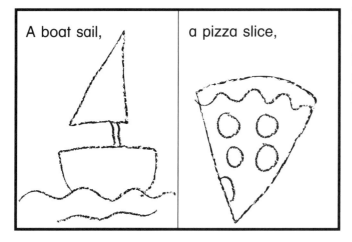

A boat sail,

a pizza slice,

Individual: Mask the illustrations on a copy of a booklet; then copy the page to make a class supply. Read aloud the text on each page and have youngsters draw pictures to match it. **Drawing shapes**

Center: Cut apart copies of two or more different shape booklets and mix the pages. A student sorts the pages by shape. **Sorting shapes**

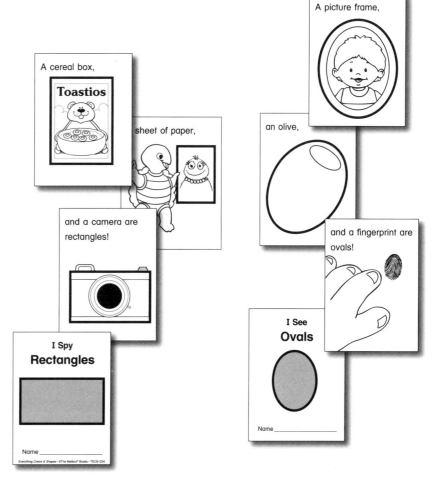

A cereal box,

Toastios

a sheet of paper,

and a camera are rectangles!

I Spy
Rectangles

Name _____

A picture frame,

an olive,

and a fingerprint are ovals!

I See
Ovals

Name _____

Turtle Tracing Page

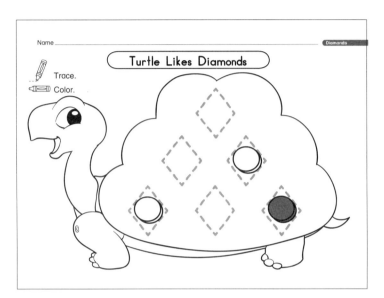

Partners: Give each pair of students a copy of a tracing page, two different-colored game markers, and a set of shape cards. Player 1 chooses a card and names the shape. If he is correct, he places a marker on the turtle. If he is incorrect, his turn is over. Player 2 takes a turn in the same manner. When a player pulls a card that matches the shape on the turtle, he puts an extra marker on the turtle's shell. When each shape on the shell is covered, the players count their markers. **Shape identification**

Cut-and-Glue Page

Partners: Have each pair of students cut out the cards at the bottom of a page. One student takes the small shapes, and the other student takes the large shapes. Player 1 names an item that is the same shape as the focus shape and places one of his cards on the mat. Player 2 takes a turn in the same manner. Alternate play continues until each child has placed all his cards on the mat. **Shape identification**

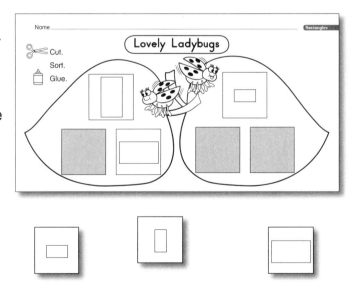